Mental Gymnastics
RECREATIONAL MATHEMATICS PUZZLES

DICK HESS

DOVER PUBLICATIONS, INC.
Mineola, New York

Bibliographical Note

Mental Gymnastics: Recreational Mathematics Puzzles is a
new work, first published by Dover Publications, Inc., in 2011.

Library of Congress Cataloging-in-Publication Data

Hess, Dick.
    Mental gymnastics : recreational mathematics puzzles / Dick Hess.
      p. cm.
    Summary: "This original compilation features new mathematical puzzles
as well as clever adaptations of traditional brainteasers. Suitable for
dedicated puzzlists ages 12 and older, it includes more than 120 challenges
involving numbers, geometry, logic, and probability, in addition to story
puzzles and playful puzzles related to games. The puzzles vary in difficulty,
and most require a bit of perseverance"— Provided by publisher.
    ISBN-13: 978-0-486-48054-1 (pbk.)
    ISBN-10: 0-486-48054-2 (pbk.)
    1. Mathematical recreations. 2. Mathematics—Problems, exercises, etc.
I. Title.
QA95.H478 2011
793.74—dc22
                                                              2011001526

Manufactured in the United States by Courier Corporation
48054203
www.doverpublications.com

To my wife, Jackie, for a lifetime of love and friendship.

CONTENTS

v

INTRODUCTION

This book is a sequel to *All-Star Mathlete Puzzles* written by me and published by Sterling Publishing Co. in 2009. The puzzles in both volumes are for the reader's enjoyment and should be passed on to others for their enjoyment as well. They are meant to challenge mathematical thinking processes including logical thought, insight, geometrical and analytical concepts, and perseverance. While most of the puzzles will succumb to pencil and paper analysis, there are some that are best tackled with a computer to search for or calculate a solution.

This book is a second helping of favorite problems I've enjoyed solving over the years. I first encountered the ideas for many of these puzzles in publications that offer problem columns or puzzle sections. These include *Crux Mathematicorum with Mathematical Mayhem, Journal of Recreational Mathematics, Pi Mu Epsilon Journal, Puzzle Corner in Technology Review,* and *The Bent.* Other puzzle ideas were introduced to me by word of mouth through a delightful community of puzzle solvers. These include Brian Barwell, Nick Baxter, Gary Foshee, Markus Götz, Wei-Hwa Huang, Hirokazu Iwasawa (Iwahiro), Steve Kahan, Scott Kim, Yoshiyuki Kotani, Andy Liu, Karl Scherer, David Singmaster, Bob Wainwright, Peter Winkler, and Nob Yoshigahara. I owe a debt of gratitude to these enthusiasts who love to share their latest challenges and listen to mine. Thanks to all who have allowed me to use their ideas and share the joy of pondering hard problems with sometimes elegant solutions.

—Dick Hess

CHAPTER 1
PLAYFUL PUZZLES

The puzzles in this chapter are relatively simple and may involve games such as bridge or chess. There is also a selection of puzzles with a whimsical element. Some can be considered to be trick problems so be on your toes.

1

SIX LOGICIANS

Six logicians have finished their dinner together. The waitress comes and asks, "Do you all want coffee?"

The first logician answers, "I don't know."
2nd logician: "I don't know."
3rd logician: "I don't know."
4th logician: "I don't know."
5th logician: "I don't know."
6th logician: "No."

To whom should the waitress serve coffee and why?

1

1 - 5

2

FIND THE SECRET MESSAGE

Find the message in the image shown below.

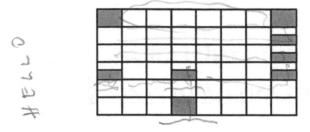

3

BRIDGE NIGHTMARE

You hold the AKQ of spades, hearts and diamonds and the AKQJ of clubs. If your opponents can pick their hands from the remaining cards what is the best contract they can make against the best defense by you and your partner?

4

COOPERATIVE BRIDGE

In the bridge hand displayed, show how South can make seven spades with the cooperation of East and West.

```
                    ♠ 85
                    ♥ Q976542
                    ♦ 5
                    ♣ 432
        ♠ K1074               ♠ Q963
        ♥ KJ8                 ♥ A10
        ♦ J103                ♦ AKQ4
        ♣ AQ10   ♠ AJ2        ♣ KJ9
                 ♥ 3
                 ♦ 98762
                 ♣ 8765
```

S
TH   4
M   9
F   12
T   16
sT   20
W   24

(28)

5

BIRTHDAY GIFT

Recently a young man was married on the first day of the month; on the last day of the month his wife gave him a chess set for his birthday. If he was married and received the chess set on the same day of the week he was born, how old was he when he got the chess set?

2/1, 2/29
MARRIED BDAY

6

FOOT RACE

Suppose you participate in 2 races with 7 other individuals on a straight track. Your job is to answer the two questions below as quickly as possible. During Race 1 you overtake the person in second place. What position are you now in? During Race 2 you overtake the person in last place, what position are you now in?

impossible

7

DEUCE POWER

A bridge partnership made game on an undoubled hand. It was noticed that each of the four deuces took a trick. What was their contract and how could it have happened? Imperfect bidding and play are allowed.

8

EXPANSION PROBLEM

Please calculate the expansion of this 26-term expression:
$E = (x-a) \times (x-b) \times (x-c) \times (x-d) ... (x-y) \times (x-z)$.

$(W-W) = 0 \quad \therefore 0$

9

CIRCULAR MATHEMATICAL WORDS

A circular word is a word with the same first and last letter. Below is a list of scrambled circular mathematical words with the first letter omitted. The first word, AREA, is solved to get you started.

1. EAR = AREA
2. ICCLY = CYCLIC
3. RISEE = SERIES
4. COIN = CONIC
5. BICU = CUBIC
6. ISPELL = ELLIPSE
7. GARBLE = ALGEBRA
8. STRICE = TRISECT
9. XMETER = EXTREME
10. TANGEIO = NEGATION
11. GOONNA = NONAGON
12. AGENTN = TANGENT
13. VINEDID = DIVIDEND
14. AXIUMM = MAXIMUM
15. GRINHAP = GRAPHING
16. INNEEET = UNINITE...
17. SIXECENT = EXISTENCE
18. MEANRIDE = REMAINDER
19. THUNDERD = HUNDREDTH
20. ANELIMIT = ELIMINATE
21. DONISTEENCC = DISCONNECT
22. SCOOPEDME = DECOMPOSE
23. METEREDIN = DETERMINE
24. BRITCUSSP = SUBSCRIPTS
25. ITISATTSC = STATISTIC
26. INNCORECT = CONCENTRIC
27. QUEENLAVIC = EQUIVALENCE
28. UNCLEANIDEO = NONEUCLID...
29. RICHCRATESITA = CHARACTERISTIC

10

WHAT MONTH?

(a) A month begins on Friday and ends on Friday. What month is it?

(b) Adding the date of the last Monday of last month to the date of the first Thursday of next month gives 38. What month is it if all dates are in the same year?

LABAAB

11

MUSICAL QUESTION

Music on the planet Alpha Lyra IV consists of only the notes A and B. Also, it never includes 3 repetitions of any sequence nor does the repetition BB ever occur. What is the longest Lyran musical composition.

12

MARY'S MOTHER

Penny
Nickel
Dime

Mary's mother has exactly four children. The first, a girl, she named Penny; the second she named Nickel and the third she named Dime. Do you know the name of her 4th child?

MARY

13

MISSING PIECE

The chess position shown was achieved in a legal game, though there is no presumption that either player was playing to win. A piece was removed from the square marked X.

What piece was it?

$$d = \frac{-b \pm \sqrt{4ac - b^2}}{2}$$

14

$\left(\frac{1}{6}\right)^5 \qquad \frac{5}{6}$

DICEY QUESTION

You are about to roll five regular dice. You win if you roll exactly one six. You lose if you roll no sixes. Are you more likely to win than lose or are you less likely to win than lose?

$x + y = 4.05$
$xy = 4.05$

$x = 4.05 - y$
$(4.05 - y)y = 4.05$
$-y^2 + 4.05y = 4.05$
$y^2 - 4.05y + 4.05 = 0$

15

STRANGE BILL

By mistake the two bills for two mugs and three plates were multiplied instead of added, but the result is $4.05 either way. What are the prices of mugs and plates if neither item costs more than a dollar?

$\frac{One}{5} \quad \overset{9}{Two} \quad \overset{8}{Three} \quad \overset{3}{Four} \quad \overset{2}{Five} \quad \overset{6}{Six} \quad \overset{7}{Seven}$
$\overset{1}{eight} \quad nine \quad zero$
$\overset{4}{} \qquad \overset{10}{}$

16

NUMERICAL DICTIONARY

Imagine a dictionary that contains all the integers written in English (no ands) in alphabetical order.
(a) What are the first and last entries? 8 — 0
(b) What is the first entry for an odd number? 5
(c) What is the 2nd to last entry? 2
(d) What is the last odd entry? 3

17

CIGARETTE LIGHTER   CUT THE CIG

You are on a deserted island. All you have is a pocketknife, a piece of flint, a can of lighter fuel and a pack of cigarettes. How would you make a cigarette lighter?

18

NUMBER SNAKE 1

Place the numbers 1 to 42 in the squares of the 6x7 grid shown so that any two consecutive numbers are orthogonally next to each other. The numbers 11, 20 and 30 are already placed to get you started.

10	11	20	21	22	23	42
9	12	19	18	17	24	41
8	13	14	15	16	25	40
7	30	29	28	27	26	39
6	31	32	33	34	35	38
5	4	3	2	1	36	37

19

MONEY QUESTION

What is the difference between an old, crumpled and worn ten-dollar bill and a new one? *$9*

20

TOY PURCHASES

A father bought 7 toys costing 25, 27, 30, 41, 58, 87 and 95 cents. Two children received toys totaling the same value. What was that value?

21

NUMBER SNAKE 2

Place the numbers 1 to 60 in the squares of the 6x10 grid shown so that any two consecutive numbers are orthogonally next to each other. The numbers 14, 29 and 46 are already placed to get you started.

13	14	29	30	31	32	33	34	35	60
12	15	28	27	26	25	24	23	36	59
11	16	17	18	19	20	21	22	37	58
10	45	44	43	42	41	40	39	38	57
9	46	47	48	49	50	51	52	53	56
8	7	6	5	4	3	2	1	54	55

CHAPTER 2

NUMERICAL PUZZLES

Ability to calculate is a valuable asset for anyone approaching the puzzles in this chapter. Some of the calculations are quite straightforward but others take some care. Enjoy the exercise.

22

ROLLING CIRCLES

Two circular disks have radii of 12 and 14. The larger disk is held fixed while the smaller disk is allowed to roll around the outside of the larger disk without slipping. In their starting positions point P on the smaller disk coincides with point Q on the larger disk. How many rotations of the smaller disk must occur before points P and Q coincide again?

Circumference $24\,\overline{\Pi}$ 2223×7
$28\,\overline{\Pi}$ $23\,7 \times 6$

9 $\frac{N}{M} = \frac{28}{24}$

$N \times 24 = M \times 28$

23

RESISTANCE OF PI

You have six resistors. Their values are ½, 1, 1, ³⁄₂, ⁵⁄₃ and 2 ohms. Produce an electrical circuit with resistance as close to pi = 3.14159265...ohms as possible.

24

BATTING ORDER

What is our baseball team's batting order if: (a) Each jersey is numbered 1 to 9. (b) Each player's jersey number is different from his batting order position. (c) Players with even numbered jerseys have even numbered batting positions. (d) Adjacent players in the batting order have jersey numbers that differ by more than one.

25

PAIRWISE SUMS

Someone has chosen four positive integers, a, b, c and d and written five of the six sums a+b, a+c, a+d, b+c, b+d and c+d. The written sums are 25, 36, 37, 48 and 54. What are the four original numbers?

26

BRIDGE CROSSING

(a) Six men must cross a bridge. They all begin on the same side and have 31 minutes to get across. It is night and they need their one flashlight to guide them on any crossing. A maximum of two people can cross at one time. Each man walks at a different speed: Man 1 takes 1 minute to cross; Man 2 takes 3 min.; Man 3 takes 4 min.; Man 4 takes 6 min.; Man 5 takes 8 min. and Man 6 takes 9 min. A pair must walk together at the rate of the slower man's pace. Try this problem as well.

(b) There are 7 men with crossing times of 1,2,6,7,8,9,10 min. and the bridge will hold up to 3 men at a time. Cross in 25 min.

27

COMBINATION RULE 1

Find the rule for combining numbers as shown below. In the diagram 88 and 63 combine to produce 25; 9 and 25 combine to produce 16 and so forth. Use the rule to determine x.

	63	9	38	33	32	12
88	25	16	18	15	x	5

28

COMBINATION RULE 2

Find the rule for combining numbers as shown below. In the diagram 34 and 16 combine to produce 18; 32 and 18 combine to produce 14 and so forth. Use the rule to determine x.

	34	32	36	46	64	75	50	35	34
16	18	14	22	x	40	35	15	20	12

29

CROSSNUMBER PUZZLE

In the clues to this puzzle p, q, r and s are always odd primes, while x and y are greater than 1. In any given clue different letters represent different integers.

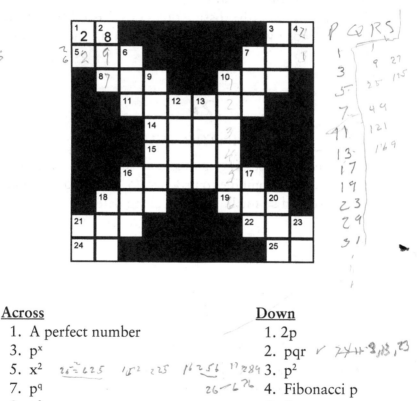

Across

1. A perfect number
3. p^x
5. x^2
7. p^q
8. $p^2 q$
10. $p^p q$
11. p^x with x>2
14. x^5

Down

1. $2p$
2. pqr
3. p^2
4. Fibonacci p
6. $2pq$
7. $=11 \bmod 13$
9. A palindrome
10. Uses the first 6 digits

15. pqrs, a palindrome
16. Odd number
18. $p^q q$
19. x^3
21. $2^p p^2 q$
22. x^2
24. One of p, q, r or s in 15 across
25. Divisible by 24 across

12. A prime
13. p
16. $2^x p^y$
17. x^3, even
18. pq
20. x^2
21. p
23. Ends in the same digit as 8 across

30

MYSTERIOUS SERIES

What is the rule for this series? What term waits the longest to make its first appearance? 20, 23, 5, 14, 20, 25, 20, 23, 5, 14, 20, 25, 20, 8, 18, 5, 5, 6, 9, 22, 5, 6, 15, 21, 18, 20, 5, 5, 14, 20, 23,...

20 / 5 , 7 , 11 , 13

31

NINE FACTORIAL

Find nine single-digit numbers other than (1,2,3,...9) with a sum of 45 and a product of 9! = 362880.

32

PANDIGITAL PRIMES

(a) Find the smallest prime number that contains each digit from 1 to 9 at least once.
(b) Now do the same for the ten digits 0 to 9.

33

COUNT THE WAYS

In how many ways can 111 be written as the sum of 3 integers in geometric progression?

34

TWELVE GOLD PYRAMIDS

Two brothers own 12 solid gold identically shaped pyramids having heights of 1, 2, 3....12 cm. How did they divide the pyramids into two sets which have the same total weight?

CHAPTER 3
GEOMETRICAL PUZZLES

Some of these puzzles are easy and some are devilishly difficult. They will sharpen your ability to think in spatial terms.

35

FOUR CUBES

In each of the four cubes shown the partitions are evenly spaced and the points A, B and C are indicated as shown. Using the simplest mathematical arguments possible to determine the angles of triangle ABC in each case.

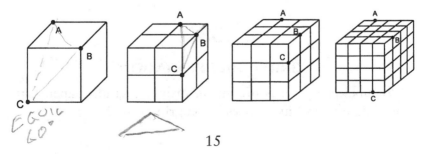

15

36

GRID POINT POLYGON

A polygon has sides in order around its perimeter of lengths 1, 2, 3,..., n. Its vertices all lie on grid points of a unit grid (that is all vertices have integer coordinates). The polygon does not cross itself, overlap itself or have any sides meeting at 0° or 180° angles.
(a) Produce such a polygon with the least number of sides.
(b) Produce such a polygon with the least odd number of sides.

37

SEVEN COOKIES

Seven circular cookies of equal size are cut from a larger circle of dough as shown. What fraction of a cookie could be made with dough scraps a+b?

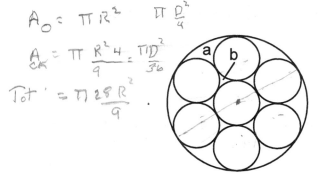

38

GRID POINT PENTAGON

A regular pentagon is drawn on ordinary graph paper. Can more than two of its vertices lie on grid points?

39

BOXED

A 1 by R rectangle is cut as shown so that the piece cut off just fits inside the remaining piece. What part, r, must be cut off to achieve this? (R<2).

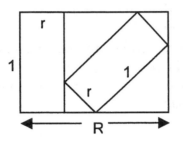

40

CUTTING A COOKIE

I'm going to cut a circular cookie into thirds (3 equal areas) by making two vertical cuts. Where should they be made?

41

DIVIDE BY THREE

The shape is half a regular hexagon. Cover it with three similar tiles (of the same shape) where no two are of the same size (two solutions known). Tiles may be turned over. Each tile must be connected and have a finite number of sides.

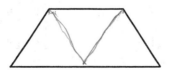

42

DIVIDE BY FOUR

The shape is half a regular hexagon. Cover it with four similar tiles (of the same shape) where:

(a) All four tiles are the same size (two solutions known).
(b) Three tiles are the same size and one is different (three solutions known).
(c) Two tiles have the same size and two have another size (two solutions known).

Tiles may be turned over. Each tile must be connected and have a finite number of sides.

43

TRIANGLE COUNT

List all isosceles triangles, other than right triangles, that use lattice points for all three vertices in:

(a) The Y-pentomino (find 16)

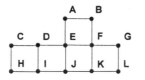

(b) The N-pentomino (find 15)

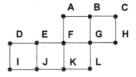

(c) The P-pentomino (find 14)

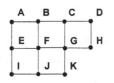

(d) The X-pentomino (find 20)

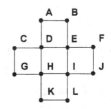

(e) The Z-pentomino (find 20)

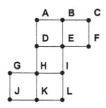

(f) The F-pentomino (find 20)

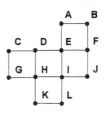

44

FISH AND GNAT

How many isosceles right triangles are determined by the vertices of
(a) the Fish, (b) the Gnat?

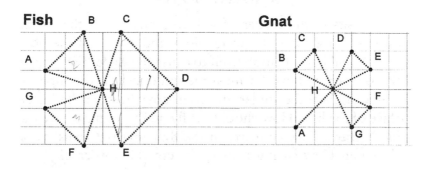

45

KOTANI'S ANT

An ant crawls along the surface of a 1x1x2 "dicube" shown.

(a) If it starts at point P, where is the farthest point from it? (It is not the opposite corner, P')

(b) What are the two points farthest apart from each other on the surface of the dicube? (the distance is greater than 3.01).

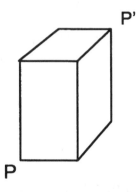

46

SPIDER AND FLY

A spider sits in the corner of a 1x2x3 box. (a) If the spider must crawl over only the walls, floor and ceiling of the box, where should a fly position itself to cause the spider the longest walk to reach it? How far must the spider crawl? (b) Suppose the fly can place the spider and itself anywhere on the inside surface of the box. How should the fly do this to maximize the spider's crawl distance to reach the fly along the walls, floor and ceiling? How far must the spider crawl in this case?

47

MINIMUM TILING

A 4x4 square is the minimum area that can be tiled by each of the I, L,T and square tetrominoes. What is the single minimum area that can be tiled in turn by each of the five tetrominoes, which now includes the N tetromino? The tetrominoes are shown here.

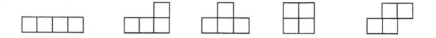

48

N SQUARES

N non-overlapping squares lie in the plane such that each one shares an edge segment of positive length with exactly three other squares. What is the smallest possible value of N? Suppose they are unit squares?

49

PACKING WINE BOTTLES

Across the horizontal bottom of a rectangular wine rack, there is room for more than three bottles (**A, B, C**) but not enough for a fourth bottle. All the bottles put into this rack are the same size with a circular cross section. Naturally, bottles **A** and **C** are laid against the sides of the rack and a second layer, consisting of just two bottles (**D, E**), holds **B** in place somewhere between **A** and **C**. Now we can lay in a third row of three bottles (**F, G, H**), with **F** and **H** resting against the sides of the rack. Then a fourth layer is held to just two bottles (**I, J**). If the gaps between the bottles are not equal in the bottom row, then the second, third, and fourth rows can slope considerably, tilting at different angles depending upon the two gaps in the bottom row. Prove that for modest arbitrary gaps in the bottom row, when the fifth row of three bottles (**K, L, M**) is added with **K** and **L** laid against the sides of the rack, the fifth row is perfectly horizontal.

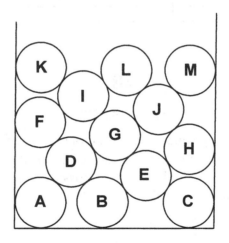

50

RIVER CROSSING

As shown, a river 10 feet wide has a right angle jog in it. You wish to cross from the south to the north side and have only two thin planks of length L and width 1 foot to help you get across. What is the smallest value for L that allows a successful plan for crossing the river?

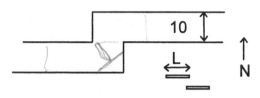

51

SHADED AREA

The triangle shown has unit area and sides trisected at points A, B, C and D as shown. What is the area of the internal quadrilateral, TUVW?

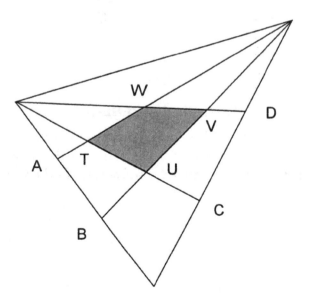

52

SLANTED ROAD

A road 10 meters wide cuts nearly diagonally across a 1 kilo-meter square as shown. What is the area of triangle ABC?

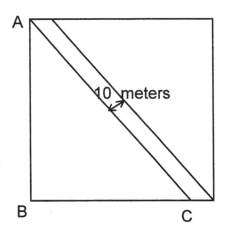

53

SPHERICAL ICEBERG

Suppose the density of ice is .9 and the density of water is 1. A spherical iceberg of radius 1 is floating in the ocean. How high is the tip of the iceberg over the surface of the water?

54

TRIANGLE TO SQUARE

The shape shown consists of 36 unit squares. Cut it into three pieces that fit together to form a square.

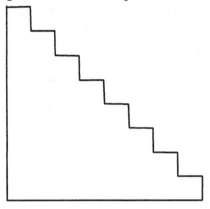

55

TRIFURCATION PROBLEM

The figure is made up of 36 unit squares. Divide it into three identical pieces. Turning pieces over is permitted.

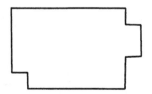

56

UNIQUE DOMINO FILLING

A 3x4 rectangle can be tiled with six dominoes. If one domino is placed in the position shown, then the other five dominoes can complete the rectangle in only one way. Place two dominoes in a 5x6 rectangle so that the other 13 can complete the tiling in only one way.

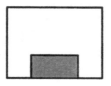

57

MINIMUM CUT LENGTH

Find the minimum cut length to dissect a unit sided equilateral triangle into four parts of equal area if:
(a) only straight line cuts are allowed.
(b) the cuts can be any shape.

CHAPTER 4

LOGICAL PUZZLES

Logical deduction is being tested for in these puzzles. Enjoy your workout.

58

ONE COUNTERFEIT COIN

You are holding a true coin and are told that among five coins on the table one is counterfeit. The counterfeit is heavier or lighter than a true coin. Find the counterfeit in two weighings using a simple two-pan balance.

59

TWO COUNTERFEIT COINS

You have seven coins among which you know there are two identical counterfeit coins each heavier than a true coin by the same amount. Find the counterfeits in three weighings using a simple two-pan balance.

60

LOGICAL HATS 1

There are five slips of paper with the number 7 written on three of them and the number 11 on the other two. Three of the slips go on the hats of logicians A, B and C in some order; the other two slips remain hidden. Each logician can see the numbers on the others' hats but not his own. The logicians are error-free in their reasoning and have all the information given so far. They are asked in turn to identify their number.

A: "I don't know my number."
B: "I don't know my number."
What number is on C?

61

ELVES AND TROLL

You are one of 50 elves trapped by a troll. He will bring all of you into a dark room, put one of 50 different cards from a standard deck of 52 playing cards on each of your foreheads, then turn on the light and ask you each in turn, "What card is on your forehead?" You see the cards on all foreheads but your own and hear the answers of those before you but when you are questioned you may only respond with the name of a card. Those who say the name of their card go free. If you are allowed to confer with the other elves ahead of time what strategy should you devise that allows the maximum number of elves to be released?

62

FOUR BLOKES WITH HATS

There are 4 blokes (A, B, C & D), who are all buried up to their necks in the ground. They cannot move, turn around, look up or down, and cannot use their hands or feet. They are all about to get shot, unless one of them (it doesn't matter who) shouts out the color of his own hat to the executioner. They cannot see their own hats. A & B are blindfolded so they see nothing. C is positioned so he can see only B; D is positioned so he can see only B & C. They each know that there are 2 black hats and 2 white hats. If they call out anything but the right answer they all get shot. After 1 minute one of them shouts out the correct answer. Which one calls out, and how does he know the color of his own hat?

63

FIVE BLOKES WITH HATS

There are 5 very intelligent logicians who know all the conditions of this problem. They are all buried up to their necks in the ground. They cannot move, turn around, look up or down, and cannot use their hands or feet. They are all about to get shot, unless one of them (it doesn't matter who) shouts out the color of his own hat to the executioner. They are buried in a circle in such a way that each can see all the other's hats except the one immediately behind them. The executioner randomly picks a hat for each prisoner from 3 black hats, 2 red hats and 1 white hat in a basket; one hat remains unseen. What color hat is shouted out? Show how the prisoners can always survive.

64

KNIGHTS AND KNAVES

(a) An island has 6 inhabitants: 3 Knaves (who always lie), 1 Knight (who always tells the truth) and 2 Normals (who sometimes lie and sometimes tell the truth). They are indistinguishable by their appearance. Can you determine who the Knight is by asking "yes" or "no" questions?

(b) Suppose there are 3 Knaves, 4 Normals and 2 Knights on the island?

65

SUM AND PRODUCT 1

Positive integers x and y, both greater than 1 but not necessarily different, are chosen. Their product is written on the hat of logician A and their sum is written on the hat of logician B. They can see the numbers on the other's hat but not on their own. The logicians are error-free in their reasoning and have all the information given so far. They make statements as follows.

B: "I don't know my number."
A: "I now know my number."
What numbers are on A and B?

66

SUM AND PRODUCT 2

Positive integers x and y, both greater than 1 but not necessarily different, are chosen. Their product is written on the hat of logician A and their sum is written on the hat of logician

B. They can see the numbers on the other's hat but not on their own. The logicians are error-free in their reasoning and have all the information given so far. They make statements as follows.

B1: "I don't know my number."
A1: "I don't know my number."
B2: "I don't know my number."
A2: "I don't know my number."
B3: "I don't know my number."
A3: "I now know my number."

What numbers are on A and B?

67

SUM AND SUM OF SQUARES

Positive integers x and y, with no common factor, are chosen. Their sum is written on the hat of logician A and the sum of their squares is written on the hat of logician B. They can see the numbers on the other's hat but not on their own. The logicians are error-free in their reasoning and have all the information given so far. They make statements as follows.

A1: "I don't know my number."
B1: "I don't know my number."
A2: "I don't know my number."
B2: "I don't know my number."
A3: "I don't know my number."
B3: "I don't know my number."
A4: "I don't know my number."
B4: "I don't know my number."
A5: "I now know my number."

What numbers are on A and B?

68

SUM AND PRODUCT 3

Integers x>0 and y>1, but not necessarily different, are chosen. Their product is written on the hat of logician A and their sum is written on the hat of logician B. They can see the numbers on the other's hat but not on their own. The logicians are error-free in their reasoning and have all the information given so far. They make statements as follows.

A1: "There is no way you can know the number on your hat."
B1: "I now know my number."
A2: "I now know my number and the sum of the numbers on our hats is under 300."

What numbers are on A and B?

69

SUM AND PRODUCT 4

Integers x>1 and y>1 are chosen such that they have no common factor other than 1. Their product is written on the hat of logician A and their sum is written on the hat of logician B. They can see the numbers on the other's hat but not on their own. The logicians are error-free in their reasoning and have all the information given so far. One of them says to the other, "You cannot know the number on your hat." The other responds, "I now know my number and yours is 1890." What numbers are on A and B?

70

THREE LOGICIANS

Each of logicians A, B, and C wears a hat with a positive integer on it. The number on one hat is the sum of the numbers on the other two. They see the numbers on the other two hats but not their own. The logicians are error-free in their reasoning and have all the information given so far. They are asked in turn to identify their number.

A1: "I don't know my number."
B1: "I don't know my number."
C1: "I don't know my number."
A2: "I don't know my number."
B2: "I don't know my number."
C2: "My number is 360360."

What number combinations are possible for A and B?

71

BLIND LOGIC

Each of logicians A, B, and C wears a hat with a single digit from 0 to 9 on it. In some order they are the digits of a square from 10^2 to 31^2. A and C can see the numbers on the other two hats but not their own. B is blind. The logicians are error-free in their reasoning and have all the information given so far. After being asked to deduce their numbers there is quite a long silence after which B announces, "I know my number." What is on B and what is possible for the numbers on A and C?

72

BELL RINGER

Each of logicians A and B wears a hat with a single integer from 0 to 19 written on it, such that the sum of the integers is either 6, 11, or 19. A bell rings every so often and after each ring all logicians who know their number announce it and share a prize. No one knows his number until after the eleventh ring, when A announces his number and wins the prize. What numbers are on A and B?

73

COUNTERFEIT STACK?

You have three stacks of five coins each and an accurate one-pan pointer scale. True coins weigh 20 gm each. All the coins in any one stack weigh the same. You are told that no more than one of the three stacks has all counterfeit coins weighing either 17 gm, 18 gm or 19 gm. In one weighing on the pointer scale determine if there is a stack of counterfeits and what their weight is.

74

COUNTERFEIT STACKS 1

You have five stacks of 16 coins each and an accurate one-pan pointer scale. True coins weigh 10 gm each. All the coins in any one stack weigh the same. You are told that no more than three of the five stacks have all counterfeit coins weighing 9 gm. In one weighing on the pointer scale, determine which stacks, if any, have counterfeits.

75

COUNTERFEIT STACKS 2

You have four stacks of seven coins each and an accurate two-pan pointer scale, which shows the signed difference (if any) between whatever (if anything) is loaded upon the two pans. All the coins in any one stack weigh the same. You are told that two stacks have 10 gm coins and two stacks have 9 gm coins. In one weighing on the pointer scale determine which stacks are which. Use the fewest coins necessary.

76

COUNTERFEIT STACKS 3

You have 17 stacks of three coins each and an accurate two-pan pointer scale, which shows the signed difference (if any) between whatever (if anything) is loaded upon the two pans. All the coins in one stack weigh the same but are different from a true coin by an amount less than 6 gm. True coins weigh an unknown whole number of grams each. In two weighings on the pointer scale find the counterfeit stack and the weight of a true coin.

CHAPTER 5

ANALYTICAL PUZZLES

The puzzles in this chapter will exercise your ability to mathematically analyze many different situations. Work up a good sweat here.

77

COMPOUND ROOTS

Simplify $x = (2+10/\sqrt{27})^{1/3} + (2-10/\sqrt{27})^{1/3}$.

78

ISLAND HOPPING

Imagine you are on a remote island with n identical airplanes and an unlimited supply of fuel and pilots. Each airplane can go a unit distance on a full tank. Aircraft all fly at the same

constant speed, can refuel each other instantly and consume fuel at the same constant rate. You wish to get all airplanes safely to a nearby island which also has an unlimited supply of fuel. For one airplane the destination island can be no farther than one unit from the home island. For two airplanes, p1 and p2 can fly out a distance of ⅓, p1 can be topped off and fly a total of ⁴⁄₃ before running out, while p2 returns to the home island safely. Then p1 can refuel, fly toward p2 a distance of ⅓ and bring both aircraft safely to the destination island. How far can the islands be apart for:
(a) three aircraft?
(b) four aircraft?

79

CIRCUMNAVIGATION

Imagine you are on a remote island with n identical airplanes and an unlimited supply of fuel and pilots. Each airplane can go a unit distance on a full tank. Aircraft all fly at the same constant speed, can refuel each other instantly and consume fuel at the same constant rate. Suppose you are on a spherical planet that is completely ocean except for the island. You wish to allow one airplane to safely circumnavigate the planet, flying over both the north and south poles before returning safely to the island. All other airplanes must safely return to the island as well. For one aircraft the circumference can be no more than 1 unit. For two aircraft the circumference can be no more than ⁵⁄₃ units. What is the largest circumference the planet can have and still allow
(a) three aircraft to refuel each other and get one to safely circumnavigate the planet?
(b) four aircraft to refuel each other and get one to safely circumnavigate the planet?

80

COLORED POINTS

Show that all points on a circle can be colored red or blue so that no inscribed right triangle has its three vertices all of the same color.

81

CHESSBOARD COLORING

A 12x12 chessboard has alternating black and white squares. In one operation every square in a single row or column is repainted the opposite color. Can all the squares be black after a certain number of operations?

82

HOUSE NUMBERS

Upon walking down a street you notice the houses on the left are numbered $1, 4, 9,...n^2$, while on the right they are numbered $1, 16, 81,...n^4$. If the sum of the house numbers on the right side is a square multiple of the sum of the house numbers on the left side, what can n be?

83

INTEGER SOLUTIONS

Find all positive and negative integer solutions (x, y) to the equation $2xy+13x-5y-75=4x^3$.

84

TEST RESULTS

Four students A, B, C and D took a math test. A full mark is 100 and each answer (or problem) has an equal share of the mark.

A notices: "The average of the four people is 75."
B states: "I had two answers wrong."
C says: "I had four answers wrong."
D says: "I had six answers wrong."
How many correct answers did A have?

85

PALINDROME CLOCK 1

There's a 12-hour digital clock (without leading zeros) at my bedside that shows hours, minutes and seconds, and which I usually look at the moment I wake up. A few days ago, I happened to wake up at a palindrome time. That is to say the time read the same forwards or backwards such as 12:33:21 or 6:45:46. Out of interest, I waited until the next palindrome time, and noticed the interval between them. Last night I woke up briefly and the same thing happened, but the interval was exactly four times as long as in the previous case. What did the clock read when I woke up last night?

86

PALINDROME CLOCK 2

Sometime within the past three years in California I noted three palindrome numbers in succession go by in local time on my computer's 12-hour clock without leading zeros. It so happened that the interval between the second two was exactly 5 times the interval between the first two. What was the exact time and calendar date of the third palindrome time?

87

SPECIAL NUMBERS

What is special about the numbers four, six, twelve, thirty, thirty-three and thirty-six...?
(a) Having found the rule for these special numbers find the next three that are perfect squares.
(b) Find the first perfect cube in the sequence.
(c) Find the next two instances of special numbers that are the product of two distinct primes.

88

ORTHOGONAL INTEGER MEDIANS

A triangle has medians that intersect at right angles.
(a) What is the smallest such triangle with sides and two of its medians all integers?
(b) Is there such a triangle with all sides and medians integers?

89

TRILATERATION PROBLEM

A point P in the plane with an equilateral triangle ABC has distances PA=1, PB=2, PC=3. How long is the side of ABC?

90

TWO TRIANGLES

Find positive integers x, y, u, v such that $x^2+y^2 = u^2$ and $x^2-xy+y^2 = v^2$.

91

THREE INTEGER TRIANGLES

In the figure the lengths a through i are integers and the angles are multiples of θ as shown. Find the smallest possible value of i.

Case (a): if α is unrestricted.
Case (b): if $\alpha < 90°$.

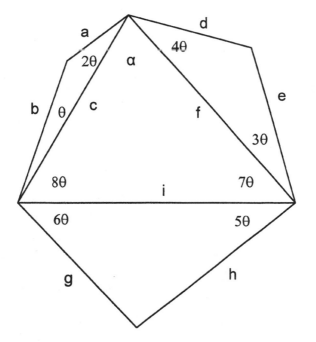

92

YOU'RE THE DOCTOR

You have an empty 5 ml vial, an empty 3 ml vial, a water supply and a single water-soluble tablet of medicine. Show how to measure out a dose (dissolved in water) of exactly (a) 10% of a tablet; (b) 13% of a tablet; (c) 1% of a tablet and (d) 7% of a tablet.

Related Problems.

For 5 ml and 4 ml vials do 50%, 61%, 74% and 38%.

For 10 ml and 7 ml vials do 40%, 10%, 50%, 25%, 29% and 19%.

For 10 ml and 9 ml vials do 30%, 40%, 50%, 5%, 41%, 57%, and 33%.

CHAPTER 6
PROBABILITY PUZZLES

The laws of probability and statistics can be a bit daunting and require you to stay on your toes. Good luck to you as you work on these puzzles.

93

AIDS TEST

A person comes from a group known to have only one person in 1000 infected with AIDS. She shows positive on an AIDS test known to be 95% correct when reading positive. What is the probability that she actually has AIDS?

94

RANDOM CHORDS

Two points are chosen randomly on a circle, C, and a chord is drawn connecting them. Two more points are chosen randomly on C and a chord is drawn connecting those two points. What is the probability that the two chords intersect inside C?

95

CUBIC TRIANGLES

Three points have been chosen randomly from the vertices of a cube. What is the probability that they form (a) an acute triangle; (b) a right triangle?

96

TYPOS

A publisher gives the proof sheets of a new book to two different proofreaders. The first reader finds 252 typos; the second finds 255. Strangely though, only 20 typos are found by both. How many typos do we expect are found by neither reader?

97

MISPLACED AVERAGES

Three families are the only occupants of an apartment building. In this building the average number of children per family is 4. Also in this building the average number of siblings per child is 5. How can this be?

98

THE ROVING ANT

(a) A lampshade has the shape of a regular octahedron and a fly is settled on one of the vertices. At t = 0 it randomly chooses one of the edges meeting at that vertex and walks along it to the adjacent vertex, arriving there at t = 1 minute. From there it immediately repeats the process, arriving at another vertex (possibly the initial one) at t = 2 minutes. If it continues this process, how long will it take the fly, on average, to arrive at the vertex diametrically opposite the starting vertex? (b) Solve for a cube. (c) Solve for a dodecahedron. (d) Solve for an icosahedron.

99

RANDOM TOSS

You are playing a game where you toss a circular disk randomly on a floor made up of square tiles. You win if the disk lands so as to cover parts of at least two tiles as long as it doesn't cover the corner of a tile. In the diagram A and B are winning positions and C and D aren't. Suppose square tiles have unit side and you get to pick the diameter of the disk. What probability of winning can you achieve and what disk diameter achieves this?

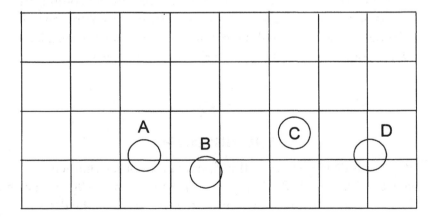

100

TUESDAY'S CHILD

Someone says to you "I have two children. At least one is a boy. He is born on Tuesday." What is the probability that both children are boys? No trick wording, just a straight probability problem. Assume boys and girls are born with equal probability and that birth on Tuesday occurs with a probability of exactly 1/7.

101

MONKEYS AND TYPEWRITERS

The infinite monkey theorem states that a monkey hitting keys at random on a typewriter keyboard for an infinite amount of time will almost surely type any given text, such as the complete works of William Shakespeare. Suppose we imagine 10^9 computers each producing 10^9 keystrokes per second for 10^9 years on virtual typewriters. Each keystroke produces with equal probability one of 100 different characters available on the typewriter. If the character strings from all the computers are joined end-to-end what is the probability that the phrase "To be or not to be" will be produced in 18 consecutive characters somewhere in the giant string of characters?

102

THE BIBLE IN PI

If we encode the letters of the alphabet and other characters as space = 00, A = 01, B = 02, C = 03 and so on up to 100 characters total then the infinite monkey theorem tells us the decimal

expansion of pi will contain any desired text of such characters in consecutive order if we just look through enough digits.
One source I found reported that the text of the Bible contains
773746 words and 3566480 letters for a total of 4340225
characters if we count the spaces between words. About how
many digits of pi will we have to examine to encounter a string
of 8680450 consecutive decimal digits that encodes the Bible
according to the above scheme?

103

FIND DICK HESS IN PI

If you are allowed to assign the letters and space in Dick Hess
to two-digit numbers of your choice, about how many digits
in the decimal expansion of pi will you need to examine before
finding the name Dick Hess encoded in pi?

CHAPTER 7

MATHDICE PUZZLES

Sam Ritchie invented the game of MathDice now being sold by ThinkFun. In MathDice, dice are thrown to determine three scoring numbers (1 to 6) and a target number to make with a mathematical expression that uses each scoring number once and only once. Each puzzle in this chapter gives scoring numbers (0 to 9) and a challenge to make a target number according to certain rules. The first set of problems uses intermediate rules in which you may use +, -, ×, ÷, exponents, decimal points, parentheses and concatenation (that is, combining two digits into another number; for instance, putting a 3 and 9 together to make 39, .93, etc.). No roots, factorials, repeating decimals or other math functions.

Two expressions are considered the same if one can be immediately derived from the other. For example, $1 \div 2^{-3}$ and 1×2^3, $6 \times .5 - 1$ and $.6 \times 5 - 1$, and $42+3$ and $43+2$ are pairs of equivalent expressions. By convention such expressions as $(.3-5)^6$ and $(5-.3)^6$ are also treated as equivalent. Bring your calculators and be prepared to consider many possibilities in these exercises.

104

MAKE 29–INTERMEDIATE RULES

The challenges:
a. Make 29 using 1, 3, and 9.
b. Make 29 using 2, 3, and 5.
c. Make 29 using 2, 2, and 6.
d. Make 29 using 3, 3, and 9.
e. Make 29 using 5, 5, and 8.
f. Make 29 in two ways using 2, 6, and 7.
g. Make 29 in two ways using 1, 1, and 3.
h. Make 29 using 3, 5, and 5.
i. Make 29 using 2, 2, and 4.

The remaining MathDice problems in this chapter use expert rules, which include the prior rules expanded to allow repeating decimals, factorials, and roots. In repeating decimals, a line is drawn under digits to indicate they repeat endlessly. So .$\underline{2}$ = .222222..., .$\underline{23}$ = .23232323..., .$2\underline{3}$ = .233333..., and .$\underline{9}$ = .999999... = 1. Concatenation, decimal points, and repeating decimals cannot be applied to expressions, only to scoring numbers. The factorial function can only be applied to integers, including expressions that equal an integer. The factorial of 0 is 1 (0! = 1). The factorials of 1 and 2 don't add anything new so they shouldn't be used. Using the square root function doesn't consume a 2, but other roots consume the digits in expressions making up the index of the root. (For instance, expressing a cube root requires the use of the digit 3 or an expression that equals 3.) Symbols in an expression may only be used a finite number of times.

105

PUZZLES WITH CONSECUTIVE SCORING NUMBERS

This set of challenges will exercise most of the combinations, concepts and themes that appear in the remaining MathDice puzzles.

a. Make 21 in two ways using 1, 2, and 3.
b. Make 35 in three ways using 1, 2, and 3.
c. Make 45 in three ways using 1, 2, and 3.
d. Make 56 in three ways using 1, 2, and 3.
e. Make 56 in five ways using 2, 3, and 4.
f. Make 70 in three ways using 2, 3, and 4.
g. Make 38 in seven ways using 2, 3, and 4.
h. Make 95 using 3, 4, and 5.
i. Make 67 in three ways using 3, 4, and 5.
j. Make 52 in two ways using 3, 4, and 5.
k. Make 58 in three ways using 4, 5, and 6.
l. Make 13 in eight ways using 4, 5, and 6.
m. Make 45 in seven ways using 4, 5, and 6.
n. Make 9 in two ways using 5, 6, and 7.
o. Make 11 in two ways using 5, 6, and 7.
p. Make 94 using 5, 6, and 7.
q. Make 40 in two ways using 5, 6, and 7.
r. Make 60 in four ways using 5, 6, and 7.
s. Make 10 in two ways using 6, 7, and 8.
t. Make 11 using 6, 7, and 8.
u. Make 12 in two ways using 6, 7, and 8.
v. Make 16 using 6, 7, and 8.
w. Make 39 using 6, 7, and 8.
x. Make 11 in two ways using 7, 8, and 9.
y. Make 67 using 7, 8, and 9.
z. Make 39 using 7, 8, and 9.

106

MAKE 75

In all cases the challenge is to make 75 from the scoring numbers. Expert rules apply here, as explained on page 49.

a. Make 75 using 5, 8, and 8.
b. Make 75 in two ways using 5, 6, and 6.
c. Make 75 using 2, 2, and 5.
d. Make 75 in two ways using 0, 5, and 6.
e. Make 75 in five ways using 1, 5, and 5.
f. Make 75 in six ways using 1, 2, and 5.
g. Make 75 in four ways using 3, 5, and 8.
h. Make 75 in four ways using 2, 4, and 9.

107

TARGETS BY 10s

For this workout each target number is a multiple of 10. Expert rules apply, as explained on page 49.

a. Make 20 using 1, 1, and 8.
b. Make 60 in two ways using 2, 2, and 2.
c. Make 70 in two ways using 2, 4, and 8.
d. Make 100 in three ways using 4, 6, and 7.
e. Make 50 using 4, 8, and 8.
f. Make 30 using 0, 6, and 7.
g. Make 90 using 2, 2, and 5.
h. Make 100 in two ways using 2, 3, and 7.
i. Make 70 in two ways using 3, 5, and 5.
j. Make 80 in three ways using 3, 7, and 9.
k. Make 30 in five ways using 4, 6, and 7.
l. Make 90 in two ways using 5, 5, and 7.
m. Make 40 in two ways using 6, 6, and 8.

n. Make 90 in two ways using 5, 8, and 8.
o. Make 20 in two ways using 0, 3, and 8.
p. Make 90 using 0, 5, and 7.
q. Make 50 in six ways using 1, 3, and 4.
r. Make 100 in four ways using 2, 3, and 5.
s. Make 90 in three ways using 2, 5, and 8.
t. Make 90 using 3, 4, and 7.
u. Make 90 using 2, 6, and 7.
v. Make 60 in four ways using 4, 6, and 7.
w. Make 70 using 5, 7, and 9.
x. Make 60 using 0, 3, and 8.
y. Make 30 using 1, 1, and 7.
z. Make 90 in two ways using 2, 3, and 7.
aa. Make 80 in two ways using 3, 6, and 7.
bb. Make 60 in five ways using 4, 7, and 9.
cc. Make 100 in four ways using 4, 8, and 9.
dd. Make 50 in five ways using 2, 5, and 8.
ee. Make 0 in two ways using 1, 5, and 8.
ff. Make 100 using 1, 4, and 7.

108

MAKE 29–EXPERT RULES

In all cases the challenge is to make 29 from the scoring numbers. Expert rules apply here, as explained on page 49.
a. Make 29 using 2, 5, and 7.
b. Make 29 using 6, 9, and 9.
c. Make 29 using 1, 5, and 8.
d. Make 29 using 5, 8, and 8.
e. Make 29 in two ways using 2, 7, and 9.
f. Make 29 using 0, 7, and 9.
g. Make 29 using 1, 6, and 9.

h. Make 29 in two ways using 2, 4, and 6.

i. Make 29 using 0, 3, and 8.

j. Make 29 in four ways using 2, 6, and 9.

k. Make 29 using 5, 6, and 6.

l. Make 29 using 3, 6, and 8.

m. Make 29 in two ways using 3, 4, and 7.

n. Make 29 using 0, 5, and 7.

o. Make 29 using 1, 1, and 2.

p. Make 29 in three ways using 0, 5, and 9.

q. Make 29 in five ways using 5, 6, and 9.

r. Make 29 in three ways using 2, 4, and 8.

s. Make 29 in five ways using 2, 4, and 4.

t. Make 29 in two ways using 5, 6, and 8.

u. Make 29 in ten ways using 4, 5, and 8.

109

HEAD-SPLITTING MATHDICE PUZZLES

Another set of over 50 MathDice problems to tackle. Expert rules apply, as explained on page 49.

a. Make 32 in two ways using 1, 3, and 7.

b. Make 41 using 1, 1, and 7.

c. Make 84 using 1, 3, and 3.

d. Make 43 in two ways using 1, 4, and 5.

e. Make 67 using 1, 5, and 5.

f. Make 16 in two ways using 1, 6, and 6.

g. Make 16 using 1, 6, and 7.

h. Make 57 using 2, 2, and 3.

i. Make 76 in three ways using 2, 3, and 8.

j. Make 45 in two ways using 2, 4, and 8.

k. Make 26 using 2, 5, and 7.

l. Make 22 using 2, 6, and 7.

   m. Make 32 in two ways using 2, 6, and 7.
   n. Make 23 using 2, 6, and 8.
   o. Make 27 using 2, 7, and 7.
   p. Make 66 using 3, 3, and 3.
   q. Make 19 in three ways using 3, 3, and 5.
   r. Make 23 using 3, 3, and 7.
   s. Make 27 in three ways using 1, 7, and 8.
   t. Make 95 using 3, 4, and 8.
   u. Make 28 in two ways using 3, 7, and 8.
   v. Make 32 using 3, 9, and 9.
   w. Make 58 using 4, 4, and 7.
   x. Make 45 using 4, 6, and 7.
   y. Make 87 using 4, 6, and 8.
   z. Make 84 in three ways using 4, 7, and 7.
  aa. Make 47 in four ways using 4, 7, and 9.
  bb. Make 76 using 4, 7, and 9.
  cc. Make 82 in two ways using 4, 8, and 9.
  dd. Make 84 in four ways using 4, 8, and 9.
  ee. Make 66 using 5, 5, and 5.
   ff. Make 56 using 5, 6, and 6.
  gg. Make 13 using 5, 7, and 7.
  hh. Make 27 in two ways using 6, 6, and 7.
   ii. Make 13 using 6, 6, and 8.
   jj. Make 35 using 7, 7, and 8.
  kk. Make 55 using 6, 7, and 9.
   ll. Make 49 using 0, 3, and 3.
 mm. Make 31 in two ways using 0, 3, and 8.
  nn. Make 41 using 0, 4, and 8.
  oo. Make 4 in two ways using 0, 6, and 7.
  pp. Make 32 using 0, 7, and 8.
  qq. Make 57 in two ways using 1, 4, and 5.
   rr. Make 92 using 1, 4, and 5.
   ss. Make 54 in three ways using 1, 4, and 7.

tt. Make 68 using 1, 5, and 9.

uu. Make 32 using 1, 6, and 6.

vv. Make 81 using 1, 7, and 8.

ww. Make 56 using 3, 3, and 9.

xx. Make 22 using 6, 6, and 6.

110

BRAIN-SHATTERING MATHDICE PUZZLES

A set of difficult MathDice problems offered to provide a full mental workout. These puzzles are intended to be the most challenging with three scoring numbers. Expert rules apply, as explained on page 49.

a. Make 67 using 8, 9, and 9.

b. Make 21 in three ways using 7, 7, and 8.

c. Make 11 in six ways using 4, 6, and 8.

d. Make 27 in three ways using 1, 1, and 7.

e. Make 33 using 0, 4, and 6.

f. Make 48 using 1, 2, and 2.

g. Make 32 in two ways using 1, 2, and 7.

h. Make 96 in two ways using 1, 2, and 9.

i. Make 96 in two ways using 1, 5, and 6.

j. Make 72 in two ways using 1, 5, and 7.

k. Make 44 using 1, 8, and 8.

l. Make 39 in two ways using 2, 4, and 6.

m. Make 84 using 2, 6, and 6.

n. Make 22 in four ways using 3, 3, and 6.

o. Make 55 using 3, 3, and 8.

p. Make 58 using 3, 4, and 7.

q. Make 42 using 3, 5, and 5.

r. Make 87 using 4, 6, and 7.

s. Make 36 in two ways using 5, 5, and 5.

  t. Make 72 using 5, 5, and 7.

  u. Make 45 in three ways using 5, 7, and 8.

  v. Make 66 using 6, 6, and 6.

  w. Make 21 in five ways using 6, 7, and 7.

  x. Make 4 in five ways using 7, 8, and 8.

  y. Make 32 in three ways using 0, 4, and 6.

  z. Make 18 in two ways using 0, 5, and 5.

aa. Make 56 in three ways using 1, 2, and 6.

bb. Make 45 in two ways using 1, 5, and 7.

cc. Make 67 using 1, 8, and 9.

dd. Make 48 in two ways using 2, 2, and 9.

ee. Make 84 using 2, 3, and 3.

 ff. Make 45 in three ways using 2, 5, and 6.

gg. Make 84 in three ways using 2, 7, and 8.

hh. Make 36 in two ways using 3, 7, and 8.

 ii. Make 56 in four ways using 4, 6, and 7.

 jj. Make 78 using 5, 5, and 6.

kk. Make 84 in four ways using 5, 6, and 6.

 ll. Make 12 in eight ways using 3, 5, and 7.

mm. Make 72 in 13 ways using 2, 3, and 8.

CHAPTER 8

MODEST POLYOMINOES

This chapter deals with the challenge to maximally cover polyomino shapes with congruent tiles, the tile's shape to be designed by the problem solver. The tiles must be identical in size and shape and may be turned over so that one is the mirror image of the other. They must not overlap each other or overhang the border of the polyomino. One engaging feature of these puzzles is that unless the coverage is 100% there is normally no easy proof that the coverage is optimal. It's possible you may discover a better answer to some of these puzzles than provided in the solutions section.

111

TWO TILES

Maximally cover the following shapes with **two** congruent and contiguous tiles. Some shapes can be covered 100%; others cannot but may use tiles that are polyominoes, have 45° diagonal cuts or cuts at other angles. A few are surprising in that a tile may be designed to get arbitrarily close to 100% coverage without actually reaching it.

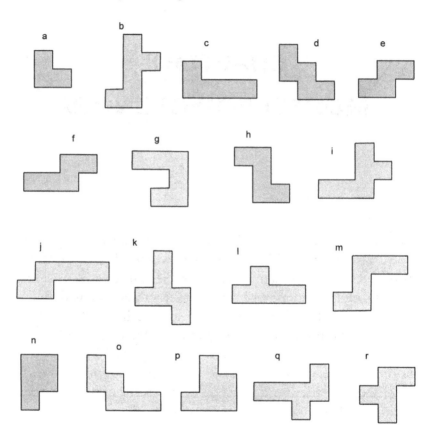

112

THREE TILES

Maximally cover the following shapes with **three** congruent and contiguous tiles.

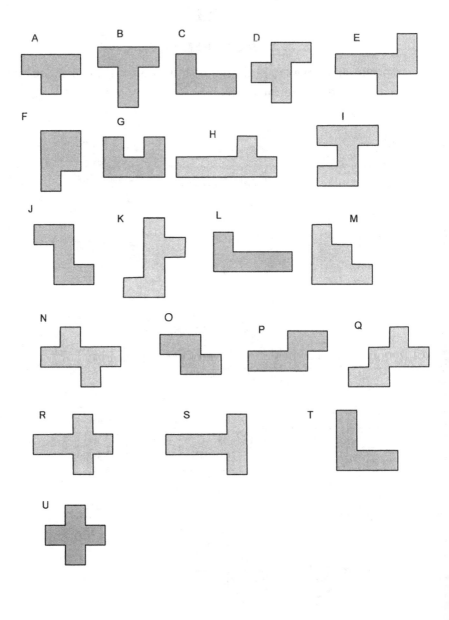

113

MULTIPLE TILES

Maximally cover the following shapes with **four or more** congruent and contiguous tiles.

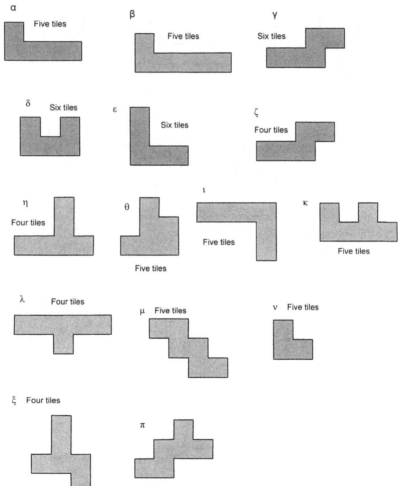

CHAPTER 9

PLAYING WITH DIGITS

Some of these puzzles are quite easy but others will challenge nearly all. Their common theme is that they all involve the manipulation of decimal digits.

114

THREE-DIGIT SQUARES

Place 13 three-digit squares in the grid shown.

115

FOUR-DIGIT SQUARES

Without using 0, place 16 digits in a 4x4 grid so that each of the four rows and four columns is a 4-digit square.

116

NUMBER SQUARE

Each letter in the 3x3 square represents a digit from 0 to 9. Determine the correspondence given that
(a) ABC and CBD are primes
(b) BBC and CDF are squares
(c) ACE and ECF are cubes

A	B	C
C	B	D
E	C	F

117

CURIOUS LICENSE PLATE

My regular racquetball opponent has a license plate whose three-digit part has the following property. Divide it by 3, reverse the digits of the result, subtract 1 and you produce the original number. What is the number and what is the next larger number (possibly with more than three digits) having this property?

118

TIME EQUATION

Fill in the boxes with the digits 0, 1, 2, 3, ...9 to make a correct multiplication equation. Each digit is used only once.

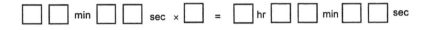

119

PI APPROXIMATION 1

A good approximation to π using just two digits is $\pi = 3.1$.

(a) Find the best approximation using two digits of your choice. You may use +, -, ×, ÷, exponents, decimal points and parentheses. No square roots or other functions are allowed.

(b) The same as (a) except square roots are allowed.

120

PI APPROXIMATION 2

A good approximation to pi using each digit 1 to 9 once is $3 + (16-8^{-5})/(97+2^4)$.

(a) Find a better approximation using each digit from 1 to 9 only once.

(b) Use the digits 0 to 9 once each to find the best approximation.

You may use +, - , ×, ÷, exponents, decimal points and parentheses. No roots, repeating decimals, factorials or other functions are allowed.

121

THREE CONSECUTIVE INTEGERS

Find three consecutive integers, the first being a multiple of the square of a prime number, the second being a multiple of the cube of a prime number and the last being a multiple of the fourth power of a prime number.

122

SIMPLE INTEGERS

Define an integer to be simple if it consists exclusively of zeros and ones in its decimal expression.

(a) Find the ten smallest simple integers divisible by 45. Let A be the average of these ten numbers. What is the value of A + 1?

(b) Find the smallest simple integer divisible by 2439.

123

THREE INTERESTING INTEGERS

(a) N_1 is a positive integer with the property that when it is increased by 10% its digital sum decreases by 11%. Find the smallest value of N_1.

(b) N_2 is a positive integer with the property that when it is increased by 10% its digital sum decreases by 10.1%. Find the smallest value of N_2.

(c) N_3 is a positive integer with the property that when it is increased by 10% its digital sum decreases by 9.99%. Find the smallest value of N_3.

SOLUTIONS

1

Six Logicians

Each of the first 5 logicians wants coffee so they are all uncertain whether all want coffee. The sixth logician doesn't want coffee and shouldn't be served coffee.

2

Find the Secret Message

Turn the figure 90° and view it nearly edge on to reveal the message "HELLO" in capitals.

3

Bridge Nightmare

For the most dramatic effect consider the hand shown where the bidding might go

South	West	North	East
2♠	pass	4♠	double
pass	pass!	pass	

Whatever west leads, the first 6 tricks are 3 ruffs by north and 3 by south ending in whichever hand ruffed the second trick. That hand leads its established red suit. East may ruff in and play two rounds of trumps at any time but will only get 3 tricks.

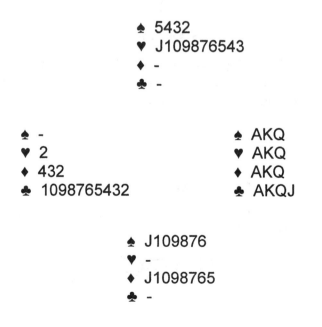

```
                    ♠ 5432
                    ♥ J109876543
                    ♦ -
                    ♣ -


  ♠ -                              ♠ AKQ
  ♥ 2                              ♥ AKQ
  ♦ 432                            ♦ AKQ
  ♣ 1098765432                     ♣ AKQJ


                    ♠ J109876
                    ♥ -
                    ♦ J1098765
                    ♣ -
```

4

Cooperative Bridge

Underlined cards in the schedule at right indicate which card took the trick.

```
        ♠ 85
        ♥ Q976542
        ♦ 5
        ♣ 432
♠ K1074          ♠ Q963
♥ KJ8            ♥ A10
♦ J103           ♦ AKQ4
♣ AQ10           ♣ KJ9
        ♠ AJ2
        ♥ 3
        ♦ 98762
        ♣ 8765
```

Trick	W	N	E	S
1	♥J	♥<u>Q</u>	♥10	♥3
2	♥K	♥2	♥A	♠<u>2</u>
3	♦3	♦<u>5</u>	♦4	♦2
4	♥8	♥<u>9</u>	♣K	♦6
5	♣A	♥<u>7</u>	♣J	♦7
6	♣Q	♥<u>6</u>	♣9	♣8
7	♣10	♥<u>5</u>	♦Q	♣7
8	♦10	♥<u>4</u>	♦K	♣6
9	♦J	♣2	♦A	♣<u>5</u>
10	♠4	♠<u>5</u>	♠3	♦9
11	♠K	♣3	♠Q	♠<u>A</u>
12	♠7	♣<u>8</u>	♠6	♦8
13	♠10	♣4	♠9	♣<u>J</u>

5

Birthday Gift

He must have been born on February 29th and was 28 years old.

6

Foot Race

In Race 1 you overtake the person in second place. You are now in second place (not first). In Race 2 you overtake the person in last place, but this is impossible, since no one can be behind the runner in last place.

7

Deuce Power

Each player must take a trick with a deuce. This is because if one player has no deuce he must be out of the led suit for the tricks taking the first three deuces so must have the suit of the fourth deuce when it is led. The defense must take at least 4 tricks. Each defender must take a trick to get the lead and another one to cash a deuce. Thus the contract must be 3 no trump. One way for all four deuces to take tricks is for each player to have 7222 distribution as shown in the diagram.

		Trick	W	N	E	S
♠ A10		1	♠J	♠A	♠5	♠3
♥ AKQJ542		2	♠K	♠10	♠6	♠4
♦ 43		3	♠2	♥4	♦7	♣4
♣ 63		4	♥7	♥A	♥9	♥3
		5	♥8	♥K	♥10	♥6
♠ KQJ9872	♠ 65	6	♠7	♥2	♦8	♠5
♥ 87	♥ 109	7	♦5	♦3	♦9	♠A
♦ 65	♦ KQJ9872	8	♦6	♦4	♦K	♦10
♣ 109	♣ 87	9	♠8	♥5	♦2	♣J
		10	♣9	♣3	♣7	♣A
♠ 43		11	♣10	♣6	♣8	♣K
♥ 63		12	♠9	♥J	♦J	♣Q
♦ A10		13	♠Q	♥Q	♦Q	♣2
♣ AKQJ542						

8

Expansion Problem

Because of the implied (x-x) term the expression calculates to E=0.

Solu

9
Circular Mathematical Words

1. EAR=AREA
2. ICCLY=CYCLIC
3. RISEE=SERIES
4. COIN=CONIC
5. BICU=CUBIC
6. ISPELL=ELLIPSE
7. GARBLE=ALGEBRA
8. STRICE=TRISECT
9. XMETER=EXTREME
10. TANGEIO=NEGATION
11. GOONNA=NONAGON
12. AGENTN=TANGENT
13. VINEDID=DIVIDEND
14. AXIUMM=MAXIMUM
15. GRINHAP=GRAPHING
16. INNEEET=NINETEEN
17. SIXECENT=EXISTENCE
18. MEANRIDE=REMAINDER
19. THUNDERD=HUNDREDTH
20. ANELIMIT=ELIMINATE
21. DONISTEENCC=DISCONNECTED
22. SCOOPEDME=DECOMPOSED
23. METEREDIN=DETERMINED
24. BRITCUSSP=SUBSCRIPTS
25. ITISATTSC=STATISTICS
26. INNCORECT=CONCENTRIC
27. QUEENLAVIC=EQUIVALENCE
28. UNCLEANIDEO=NONEUCLIDEAN
29. RICHCRATESITA=CHARACTERISTIC

10

What Month

(a) It must be February in a leap year.

(b) The first Thursday of next month must be the 7th and the last Monday of last month must be the 31st to get a total of 38. The last Thursday of this month must be the 31st so this month must be August.

11

Musical Question

The longest musical compositions without three consecutive repetitions of any sequence are AABABAABABAABAAB and its reverse.

12

Mary's Mother

Mary's <u>mother</u> has Penny, Nickel, Dime, and Mary as her children. Mary is the 4th child. Therefore the correct answer to the actual question is "yes."

13

Missing Piece

(1) Since black is in check, white made the last move.

(2) It must have been a capture and promotion of a white pawn moving to d8.

(3) Black's captured piece on d8 must have been a knight or bishop; this piece or one of black's knights must have come from a promoted black pawn.

(4) No black pieces are possible on X because a rook or queen would check white, all pawns and knights are accounted

for and the black bishop has no escape path from its home square.

(5) Black has made five captures in order to achieve the promoted pawn and current pawn position. These captures were all on squares of the same color so the piece that was removed must be a white bishop.

(6) At this stage it's clear that black's captured piece on d8 must have been a knight since a promoted bishop on g1 would have no escape path.

14

Dicey Question

The answer is no. Both probabilities are equal.

15

Strange Bill

Let m be the price of a mug and p be the price of a plate. Then $6mp = 2m+3p = 4.05$. This has two solutions with $(p, m) =$

(.60, 1.125) or (.75, .90). The second solution has both items priced under a dollar.

16

Numerical Dictionary

(a) 8 and 0. (b) 8,808,808,885. Some dictionaries might have eighteen precede eight hundred; for such dictionaries 8,018,018,885 would be the first odd number. (c) The second to last entry is two vigintillion two undecillion two trillion two thousand two hundred two. (d) The last odd entry is two vigintillion two undecillion two trillion two thousand two hundred twenty-three.

17

Cigarette Lighter

Cut a piece off and discard it.

18

Number Snake 1

As shown.

10	11	20	21	22	23	42
9	12	19	18	17	24	41
8	13	14	15	16	25	40
7	30	29	28	27	26	39
6	31	32	33	34	35	38
5	4	3	2	1	36	37

19

Money Question

Nine dollars is the difference between an old $10 bill and a new $1 bill.

20

Toy Purchases

$.58+$.95=$.25+$.41+$.87=$1.53.

?, where is the ?
27 ¢ .30 toy?

21

Number Snake 2

13	14	29	30	31	32	33	34	35	60
12	15	28	27	26	25	24	23	36	59
11	16	17	18	19	20	21	22	37	58
10	45	44	43	42	41	40	39	38	57
9	46	47	48	49	50	51	52	53	56
8	7	6	5	4	3	2	1	54	55

22

Rolling Circles

Six circumference lengths of the larger disk are equal to seven circumference lengths of the smaller disk. This distance must be traveled before P and Q again coincide. This causes the smaller disk to execute 13 full rotations. Seven come from the rotations it would accumulate on a straight path and six come from traveling around the larger disk that number of times.

23

Resistance of Pi

The resistance between points P and Q in the circuit below is 355/113, which differs from pi by about 2.668×10^{-7}. The resistance between points P and Q of the second circuit (shown with arbitrary resistances A through E) is R = $[ACS_2+(AD+BC)E+BDS_1]/(S_1S_2-E^2)$, where S_1 = A+C+E and S_2 = B+D+E.

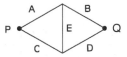

24

Batting Order

385274961 or 941638527

25

Pairwise Sums

Note that $25+48 = 36+37$, leaving 54 as the "odd one out." If we call 54 = c+d then the combinations a+c, a+d, b+c, and b+d account for 25, 36, 37 and 48 in some order. It follows that 25+48 = 73 = a+b+c+d and we now can compute a+b = 19. From the common differences 11 = 48-37 = 36-25 and 12 = 48-36 = 37-25 we can deduce that a and b differ by 11 and c and d differ by 12. Thus the four numbers are 4, 15, 21 and 23, with the first pair being a and b in some order and the second pair being c and d in some order.

26

Bridge Crossing

(a) 1 and 3 go across, 1 comes back; 8 and 9 go across, 3 comes back; 1 and 6 go across, 1 comes back; 1 and 4 go across, 1 comes back; 1 and 3 go across.

(b) 1 and 2 go across, 1 comes back; 8, 9 and 10 go across, 2 comes back; 1, 6 and 7 go across, 1 comes back; 1 and 2 go across.

27

Combination Rule 1

At first glance it appears the rule might be subtraction and x=17. But this is not right because 18 is not the difference of 38 and 16. Instead the rule is that two numbers combine to give a number that is the sum of the digits of the two numbers. Thus x=11.

63		9		38		33		32		12	
88		25		16		18		15		x		5

28

Combination Rule 2

In each case the numbers combine by summing the products of their digits. Thus x = 4x6+2x2 = 28

34	32	36	46	64	75	50	35	34
16	18	14	22	x	40	35	15	20	12

29

Crossnumber Puzzle

30

Mysterious Series

Each number is a code for a letter in English with A=1, B=2 and so on. The series then references itself. The number 24 appears as the 120th term, the final term to make its first appearance.

31

Nine Factorial

The other set of numbers is 1, 2, 4, 4, 4, 5, 7, 9, and 9.

32

Pandigital Primes

(a) 1123465789. (b) 10123457689.

33

Count the Ways

Let x be the first number in the sum and let r be the geometric ratio. Then $111 = x + xr + xr^2$, where x, xr and xr^2 are all integers. For a given x the ratio $r = (-x \pm \sqrt{(444x - 3x^2)})/(2x)$. We must try each x from 1 to 148 and test whether xr is integer for both signs in the expression for xr. The result is that there are 17 ways:
(1, 10, 100), (1, -11, 121), (27, 36, 48), (27, -63, 147), (37, 37, 37), (37, -74, 148), (48, 36, 27), (48, -84, 147), (100, 10, 1), (100, -110, 121), (111, 0, 0), (111, -111, 111), (121, -11, 1), (121, -110, 100), (147, -63, 27), (147, -84, 48), (148, -74, 37).

34

Twelve Gold Pyramids

To get the weights to balance we need the sum of the cubes of the heights to balance for the two sets of pyramids. This is accomplished with $1+8+64+512+729+1728 = 27+125+216+343+1000+1331$.

35

Four Cubes

A plane through ABC in the 1-cube produces an equilateral triangle so all angles are 60°. A plane through ABC in the 2-cube produces a regular hexagon as it intersects the cube faces so angles A and C are each 30° and angle B is 120°. A plane through ABC in the 3-cube produces a hexagon with alternating sides of single length and double length. Angle B is 120° and angles A and C are defined by $\sin^2 A = 3/7$ and $\sin^2 C = 3/28$. In the 4-cube notice that $AB^2 = BC^2 = 18$ and $AC^2 = 36$. Thus ABC is an isosceles right triangle with $A = C = 45°$ and $B = 90°$.

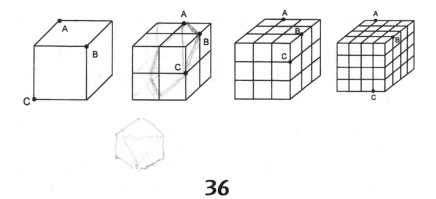

36

Grid Point Polygon

The first 4 legs (lengths 1, 2, 3, 4) must be connected by right angle bends. Characterize the legs as vectors and define leg 1 as (1,0). Then leg 2 will be (0,2), which can be added to or subtracted from the first leg to get the vertex at the end of leg 2. The next two legs will be (3,0) and (0,4) to be added or subtracted at will. There can be no four-sided solution since the x-components (1 and 3) cannot add to zero.

Because five can be the side of a Pythagorean triangle (3-4-5) leg 5 can take 10 possible directions from the end of leg 4. These come from the vectors (5,0), (3,4) and (4,3) with arbitrary signs on the components. A solution with five sides would require the first four sides to add to one of these ten vectors. A 5-sided solution is impossible because any sum of the first four legs gives even numbers for both the x and y coordinates. A 6-sided solution is impossible for the same reason since the sum of all legs other than leg 5 gives a vector with even coordinates for both components.

If there is a 7-sided solution leg 7 must be (0,7) or (0,-7) so as to meet leg 1 properly and leg 6 must be (6,0) or (-6,0). The sum of all legs but leg 5 will add or subtract 1, 3 and 6 in the x direction and add or subtract 2, 4 and 7 in the y direction. We cannot get any of the 10 vectors for leg 5 with these numbers so a 7-sided solution is impossible.

With eight legs there are finally enough possibilities to come up with three solutions shown here.

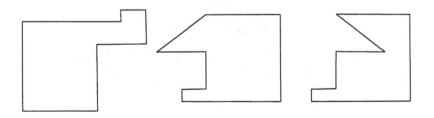

For a 9-sided solution we must have 1, 3, 6 and 8 contributing in the x direction and 2, 4, 7 and 9 contributing in the y direction in an attempt to add to one of the ten vectors possible for leg 5. A 9-sided solution is impossible because any sum of these eight legs gives even numbers for both the x and y coordinates.

The 11-sided swan and woodpecker shaped polygons shown are two examples of a polygon with the least odd number of sides possible. For interest the 15-sided Texas-shaped polygon is shown as well.

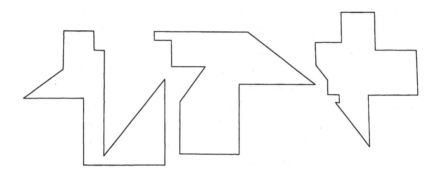

37

Seven Cookies

The large circle has 9 times the area of each small circle so that $6(a+b) = 2$ cookies and $a+b =$ one third of a cookie.

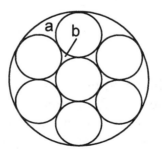

38

Grid Point Pentagon

Assume that three vertices do fall on grid points. The triangle they form will always include a vertex with an angle of 36° as shown. Place that vertex at the origin and suppose the other two vertices of the triangle are at grid points (a, b) and (c, d), where a, b, c and d are integers. Then $\cos^2 36° = (ac+bd)^2/((a^2+b^2)\times(c^2+d^2))$. But $\cos^2 36°$ is irrational and therefore cannot be the ratio of two integers. This contradiction proves that three vertices of the regular pentagon cannot lie on grid points.

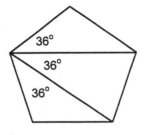

39

Boxed

From the figure $\sin\theta + r\cos\theta = 1$ and $\cos\theta + r\sin\theta = R-r$. It follows that $r = (1-\sin\theta)/\cos\theta = (R-\cos\theta)/(1+\sin\theta)$ from which $R = 2\cos\theta$ and $r = [2-\sqrt{(4-R^2)}]/R$.

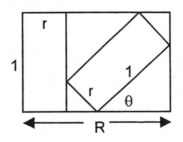

40

Cutting a Cookie

Let the cookie have unit radius so its area is π. Then the cut in the figure must be such that $A = \theta - \sin\theta\cos\theta = \pi/3$. This occurs at $\theta = 74.63708276...$degrees. The cut passes within $x = \cos\theta = .264932083...$of the center of the cookie.

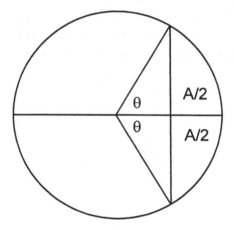

41

Divide by Three

Solutions are shown with approximate line lengths indicated. Three sides of the half hexagon are unit length.

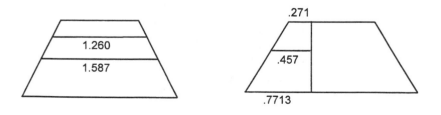

42

Divide by Four

Solutions are shown with approximate line lengths indicated. Three sides of the half hexagon are unit length.

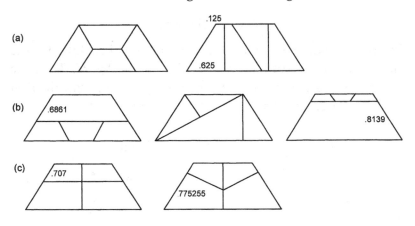

43

Triangle Count

(a) Y(16): ACG, ACI, ACJ, ADK, AFI, AGJ, AGK, AIK, BCK, BDJ, BDK, BEL, BGJ, BJL, CGJ, EHL

(b) N(15): ACL, ADH, ADJ, ADK, AEL, AGJ, AHK, AHL, AJL, BDL, BEK, BEL, BHK, CFL, DHK

(c) P(14): ACJ, AGI, AGJ, AHI, BDK, BEK, BGI, BHJ, BHK, BIK, CEJ, CEK, CHJ, DFK

(d) X(20): ACI, AEG, AFH, AFI, AGI, BCH, BCI, BDJ, BFH, BHJ, CEK, CIK, DFL, DGL, DJK, DJL, EGK, EGL, EJK, FHL

(e) Z(20): ACI, ACL, AEG, AFH, AFI, AGI, AJL, BFH, BFJ, CDI, CDJ, CGK, CIJ, DFL, DGL, DIJ, DJL, EGK, EGL, FHL

(f) F(20):   ACH, ACI, ADJ, AFH, AHJ, BCJ, BCL, BDI, BDJ,
             BGK, CEK, CIK, DFL, DGL, DJK, DJL, EGK, EGL,
             EJK, FHL

44

Fish and Gnat

The points that make up the Gnat are identical to those for the
Fish except for a rotation and scaling of the figure. Thus the
number of triangles is the same for both problems. For the Fish
there are three such triangles: ACF, BEG and CDE.

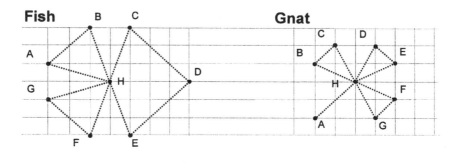

45

Kotani's Ant

The generalized schematic on the next page shows a 1xaxb
box "unfolded" to display all possible shortest paths from
a starting point P on the 1xa face of the box to a destination point Q on the opposite 1xa face. The point Q' is on the
1xa face with P and directly opposite the destination point Q
(on a line through Q and the body center of the box). Q' has
coordinates p and q. The coordinates of each of the 20 images
of Q are given relative to the origin, O. The distance from P
to Q is the smallest of the distances to the 20 images. For
this problem the box is 1x1x2 and P is at the origin. (a) The
farthest point from P occurs when Q' = (¼, ¼), which puts

Q one fourth of the way along the diagonal on the 1x1 face from P'. (b) When both P and Q are allowed to vary the maximum distance between the two occurs for P = Q' = (($\sqrt{3}$-1)/2, ($\sqrt{3}$-1)/2). The two points are on the diagonal near P' and its opposite point on the 1x1 face which includes P. The distance between them is $\sqrt{(16-\sqrt{48})}$ = 3.011942358....

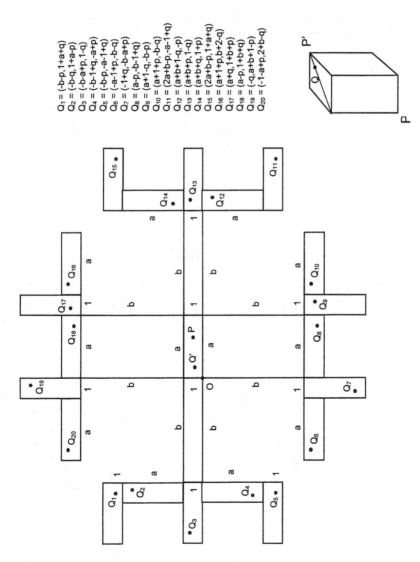

$Q_1 = (-b-p, 1+a+q)$
$Q_2 = (-b-q, 1+a-p)$
$Q_3 = (-b-a+p, 1-q)$
$Q_4 = (-b-1+q, -a+p)$
$Q_5 = (-b-p, -a-1+q)$
$Q_6 = (-a-1+p, -b-q)$
$Q_7 = (-1+q, -b-a+p)$
$Q_8 = (a-p, -b-1+q)$
$Q_9 = (a+1-q, -b-p)$
$Q_{10} = (a+1+p, -b-q)$
$Q_{11} = (2a+b-p, -a-1+q)$
$Q_{12} = (a+b+1-q, -p)$
$Q_{13} = (a+b+p, 1-q)$
$Q_{14} = (a+b+q, 1+p)$
$Q_{15} = (2a+b-p, 1+a+q)$
$Q_{16} = (a+1+p, b+2-q)$
$Q_{17} = (a+q, 1+b+p)$
$Q_{18} = (a-p, 1+b+q)$
$Q_{19} = (-q, a+b+1-p)$
$Q_{20} = (-1-a+p, 2+b-q)$

46

Spider and Fly

Use the schematic of the prior problem with a = 2 and b = 3.

(a) When P is a corner of the box the farthest distance comes for Q' = (⅛, ⅛). Thus we place the fly on the far 1x2 face near the diagonally opposite corner a distance ⅛ from each edge. The spider must crawl d = $\sqrt{(325/18)}$ = 4.24918.

(b) For the two to be maximally separated place the spider and fly on opposite 1x2 faces so that P = Q' = ((5-$\sqrt{22}$)/2, .5). Each should be halfway between the edges of length 2 and .154792 from an edge of length 1. The spider must crawl d = 4.3425229. d² = 47+6$\sqrt{22}$.

47

Minimum Tiling

The 32-square donut-shaped figure shown is the smallest known region that can be tiled by each of the five tetrominoes.

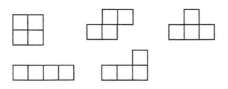

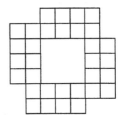

48

N Squares

The best solutions known are shown here.

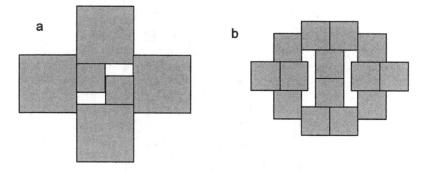

49

Packing Wine Bottles

Model the bottles as circles with unit radius and let the gap
between **A** and **B** be a and the gap between **B** and **C** be b. If the
lower left corner is the origin then coordinates of the centers of
the circles can be determined as follows.

A = (1,1); **B** = (3+a, 1); **C** = (5+a+b, 1); **D** = (2+a/2, 1+√(3-
a-a²/4)); **E** = (4+a+b/2, 1+√(3-b-b²/4)); **F** = (1, 1+2√(3-a-a²/4));
H = (5+a+b, 1+2√(3-b-b²/4)).

Then **D** + **E** = **B** + **G** so **G** = **D** + **E** - **B** = (3+a/2+b/2, √(3-a-a²/4)
+ √(3-b-b²/4)+1) = (**F**+**H**)/2. This shows that **F**, **G** and **H** must
lie in a straight line. Now it is clear a 180° rotation of bottles
A through **E** about the center of **G** puts them exactly in the
positions of bottles **I** through **M**, showing that **K**, **L** and **M**
must lie on a horizontal line. The gaps a and b must be smaller
than 2√3-2 = 1.464106...to avoid overlaps.

Interestingly enough the same approach shows that for a stack of bottles with four on the bottom row with suitable gaps, the 7th row of bottles is also horizontal.

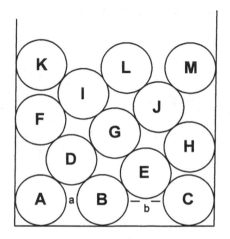

50

River Crossing

In the figure the oblique lines each have a length of $20\sqrt{2}/3 = 9.42809$ feet. If these lines are interpreted as the diagonals of the planks then the planks can be almost as short as $L = \sqrt{(791)}/3 = 9.3749074$ feet.

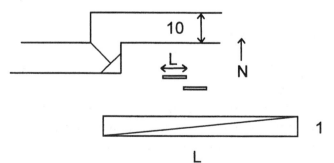

51

Shaded Area

Without loss of generality we may take the triangle to be right isosceles with unit side. The four lines bordering the shaded region have the following equations. WT: y = -3x+1; VU: y = -3x/2+1; TU: 3y = -x+1; WV: 1.5y = -x+1. From these lines the coordinates of T, W and V are T=(¼,¼); W=(⅐,⁴⁄₇); V= (⅖,⅖). The area of TUVW = |(T-W)**x**(T-V)| = 9/140. Since the triangle has an area of ½, the shaded fraction is 9/70 =.12855142857...

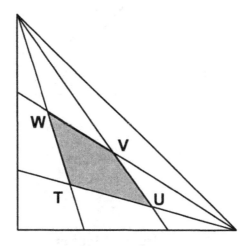

52

Slanted Road

The square is 1000 meters on a side. The area of ABC = 500(1000-d); tanθ = 1000/(1000-d) = sinθ/cosθ; sinθ = 10/d leads to 1000sinθ-1000cosθ = 10. Thus sin2θ = 2sinθ cosθ = 1-(sinθ-cosθ)^2 = .9999 and cos2θ = -.014141782. From this d = 14.04318638... meters and the area of ABC is 492978.4068... square meters.

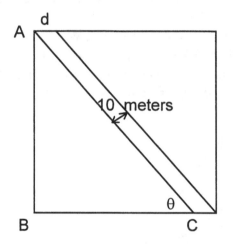

53

Spherical Iceberg

The volume of a spherical cap of height h above the waterline is πh^2(r-h/3) for a sphere of radius r. For ice of density .9 floating in water of density 1 this volume will be one tenth of the total volume of the sphere, which is 4πr^3/3. For a unit radius this requires h^3 - 3h^2 + $\frac{2}{15}$ = 0 and h = .39160020649...

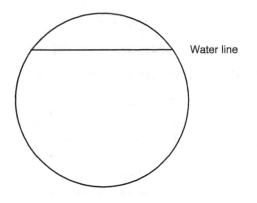

Water line

54

Triangle to Square

Start and end positions are shown.

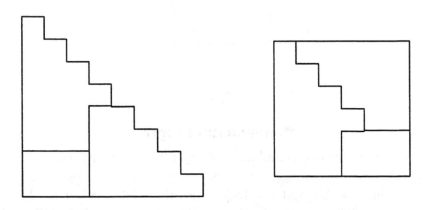

55

Trifurcation Problem

Division into three identical tiles is shown.

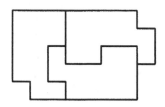

56

Unique Domino Filling

Placing two dominos as shown forces placement of all others to fill the 5x6 rectangle.

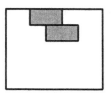

57

Minimum Cut Length

(a) Cut a unit sided equilateral triangle into four parts of equal area if only straight line cuts are allowed. In the figure define $x = AD$ and $y = DQ$. From this $QR = u = 1-x-\sqrt{3}y$ and $QW = v = \sqrt{3}x/2 - y/2$. The four areas ATQP, CPQRS, QTUR and BSRU must each equal $\sqrt{3}/16$. From this it follows the length $z = TW = \sqrt{3}/(16v) - u$. Define $f = DP$. Then the area constraints require $fy = \sqrt{3}/16 - xy - v/2 - uv$. The total cut length is $L = 2QT + 2PQ + QR = 2\sqrt{(v^2 + z^2)} + 2\sqrt{(y^2 + f^2)} + u$. Vary x and y to achieve a minimum $L = 1.310804606...$ when $x = .549792$, $y = .139546$, $u = .208508$, $v = .406361$, $z = .057889$, $f = .0178668$.

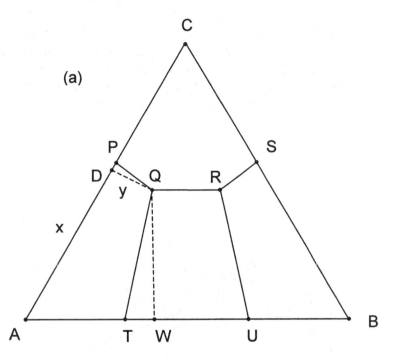

(a)

(b) Cut a unit sided equilateral triangle into four parts of equal area if the cuts can be any shape. The figure shows the approximate curved lines for minimum cut length. The minimum length is $L = 1.30511...$ Imagine the curved lines are soap films, which are known to take on the minimum length. Also known is that the curves are arcs of circles and the three arcs must meet at P and Q with 120° angles. Pick $x = AD$, $y = DQ$ and $r_1 = QC_1$ as shown. Then $QR = u = 1 - x - \sqrt{3}y$ and $QW = v = \sqrt{3}x/2 - y/2$. The angle constraints require

$\theta_2 = \theta_3 = 30°-\theta_1$. From this we compute $r_2 = v/\sin\theta_2$ and r_3 $= y/\sin\theta_3$. The area of TWQ is then $A_2 = r_2{}^2(\theta_2-\sin\theta_2\cos\theta_2)$. Similar areas for A_3 = DQP and A_1 = QGF are given by A_3 $= r_3{}^2(\theta_3-\sin\theta_3\cos\theta_3)$ and $A_1 = r_1{}^2(\theta_1-\sin\theta_1\cos\theta_1)$. The area requirements are now area PQRSC $= \sqrt{3}/16 = (\sqrt{3}/2-v)u/2+$ $(1-x)y-2A_3-2A_1$; area TURQ $= \sqrt{3}/16 = uv+2A_1+2A_2$; area APQT $= \sqrt{3}/16 = xy/2+(1-u)v/4-A_2+A_3$. The cut length is $L = 2(r_1\theta_1+ r_2\theta_3+ r_3\theta_3)$. Vary x, y and r_1 to achieve a minimum L = 1.30511...when x = .545039, y = .149684, r_1 = .393284, θ_1 = 14.40672°, u = .195701, v = .397176, r_2 = 1.477550, $\theta_2 = \theta_3$ = 15.593284°, r_3 = .556846.

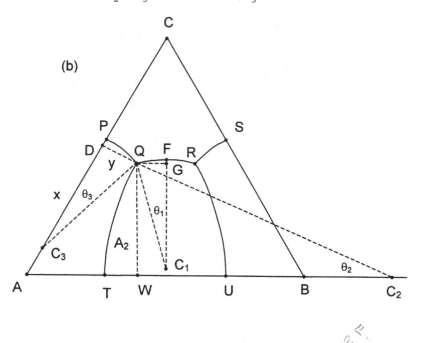

(b)

58

One Counterfeit Coin

Label the coins from A to F, with F being the true coin. In the first weighing balance B+F (right pan) against C+E (left pan).

In the second balance D+F (right pan) against B+E (left pan). If both weighings balance then coin A is fake. If the two weighings are unbalanced in opposite directions then coin B is fake. If the two weighings are unbalanced in the same direction then coin E is fake. If the first weighing balances and the second doesn't then coin D is fake. If the first weighing doesn't balance and the second does then coin C is fake.

59

Two Counterfeit Coins

Label the coins from A to G. The first table shows the weighing strategy. L means the coin is placed in the left pan; R means the coin is placed in the right pan; 0 means the coin does not participate in the weighing. Thus the first weighing is A and B versus C and D. Note that the third weighing depends on the outcomes of the first two. The notation used is that, for example, 0- would indicate in the first weighing the pans balance and in the second weighing the left pan is light.

The second table shows which coins are counterfeit depending on the outcomes of the three weighings. The outcome is indicated by how the left pan behaves in each weighing.

Coins	Weighings			
	First	Second	Third for ++, -- or -0	Third for all others
A	L	L	L	0
B	L	0	R	L
C	R	L	0	0
D	R	0	0	R
E	0	R	L	R
F	0	R	R	0
G	0	0	0	L

Outcome	Counterfeits	Outcome	Counterfeits
+++	AG	0-+	FG
++0	AB	0-0	EG
+0+	BG	0--	EF
+00	AF	-++	CG
+0-	AE	-+-	CD
+-+	BF	-0+	CE
+-0	BE	-00	DG
0++	BC	-0-	CF
0+0	AC	--+	DE
0+-	AD	---	DF
000	BD		

60

Logical Hats 1

Because A doesn't know, he cannot have seen two 11's. Because B doesn't know, and he knows A doesn't know, he cannot have seen any 11's. Thus C has a 7 on his hat.

61

Elves and a Troll

With the proper strategy all but the first elf can go free. What is needed is agreement from all that whoever goes first will be a martyr. All elves agree on a natural ordering of the cards that labels them from 0 to 51. Whoever goes first adds the numbers of the cards he can see and takes the result mod 52 (that is he divides the sum by 52 and takes the remainder). Call this result

R. He guesses the card corresponding to R. Each other elf then knows that the sum of cards they can see, leaving out the card from the first elf, will equal R if their card is added in. Thus each elf other than the first deduces his card and is set free.

62

Four Blokes with Hats

C knows the color of his hat is opposite to that of B. His reasoning is that because D has not called out, D has seen different color hats on B and C.

63

Five Blokes with Hats

The deduced color of the hat is black. Let B, R and W stand for black, red and white. They can all reason as follows. If RRW, RWR or WRR occurs next to each other anywhere around the circle whoever sees that combination will call out his hat color as B within 20 seconds. If RR, RW or WR occurs next to each other anywhere around the circle, whoever sees that combination directly in front of him will wait 20 seconds to verify he isn't wearing R or W and will then call out his hat color as B within 40 seconds. If R or W occurs directly in front of someone then he waits 40 seconds to verify he is not wearing W or R and declares his hat is B.

64

Knights and Knaves

(a) (1) Ask all inhabitants "Does 2+2=5?" Those saying yes are either Knaves or Normals (Call them Group A); those saying no are either Knights or Normals (Call them Group B). (2) To each member of group A ask about each member of Group B "Is he a Normal?" Knaves will answer yes for the Knight and no for the Normals. Since there are more Knaves than Normals in Group A, whichever member of group B gets the most yes answers is the Knight.

(b) Same as above but you must also ask each member of Group B "Is he a Knight?" about each member of Group B. All Knights will answer yes for Knights and no for Normals. The sum of yes answers from (2) above and this question will be at least 5 for each Knight and the sum of the no answers will be at least 5 for the Normals in Group B.

65

Sum and Product 1

The table shows cases for x and y with combinations eliminated by B's statement marked with a B. These are eliminated because they give a unique pair of factors for the product of x and y. The possibilities for A as seen by A are all empty cells along an upward sloping diagonal for the sum x+y. The only diagonal with a single empty cell is the one for x = 4 and y = 3 (marked by **A**). Thus B sees 12 on A's hat and A sees 7 on B's hat.

	x=2	x=3	x=4	x=5	x=6	x=7	x=8	x=9
y=2	B	B	B	B		B		
y=3		B	**A**	B		B		B
y=4								
y=5				B		B		
y=6								
y=7						B		
y=8								

66

Sum and Product 2

The table shows cases for x and y. The cells marked B1 are eliminated because they give a unique pair of factors for x×y. The cell marked A1 is next eliminated because of the remaining blank cells it has a unique value of x+y. The cell marked B2 is then eliminated because of the remaining blank cells. It has a unique value of x×y. The cells marked A2 and B3 are finally eliminated because of the remaining blank cells they have unique values of x+y and x×y. **A3** now marks the unique cell allowing A to know his number. Thus B sees 24 on A's hat and A sees 10 on B's hat.

	x=2	x=3	x=4	x=5	x=6	x=7	x=8	x=9
y=2	B1	B1	B1	B1	B2	B1	B3	
y=3		B1	A1	B1		B1		B1
y=4			A2		**A3**			
y=5				B1		B1		
y=6								
y=7						B1		
y=8								

67

Sum and Sum of Squares

In the table cells are left blank if x and y share a common factor. When x and y have no common factor, x^2+y^2 is a unique number for many choices of x and y. Cells with this characteristic are also left blank because the first statement by A eliminates them. The remaining cells where x+y is unique are then marked with B1 because B's first statement eliminates them. The remaining cells with a unique value of x^2+y^2 are then marked with A2 and the steps continued until we get to the cell marked **A5**. This is the solution so that A is looking at 530 on B's hat and B is looking at 32 on A's hat. Numbers in the cells show the value of x^2+y^2 for cases where the same value of x^2+y^2 can be reached by more than one combination of x and y.

	x=7	x=8	x=9	x=10	x=11	x=12	x=13	x=14	x=15	x=16	x=17	x=18	x=19	x=20
y=1		B1				B3	B2				B3	325		
y=2			B2										365	
y=3					A2			205		265			370	
y=4	A2						185				305		377	
y=5								221						
y=6	A3						205				325			
y=7			B1		A3						305		410	
y=8			A4		185								425	
y=9											370		442	481
y=10					221									
y=11						265	A4				377	410	445	
y=12													505	
y=13							365				425		493	**A5**

68

Sum and Product 3

In the table cells are left blank if they are inconsistent with A's first statement. The only cells consistent have a sum x+y = 11, 17, 23,... The cell marked B1, at (x,y) = (6,5) is inconsistent with B's first statement because the product of 30 could come from (x,y) = (3,10) as well. The cell marked **A2** is the solution to the problem with A looking at 17 on B's hat and B is looking at 52 on A's hat. An extension of the table shows other solutions at (x,y) = (61,4), (73,16), (111,16), (73,64),..., (556,201),...

	x=6	x=7	x=8	x=9	x=10	x=11	x=12	x=13	x=14	x=15
y=2				18						30
y=3			24						42	
y=4		21						**A2**		
y=5	B1						60			
y=6						66				
y=7					70					
y=8				72						120
y=9									126	
y=10								130		
y=11							132			

69

Sum and Product 4

A sees 149 on B and knows that B cannot know his number. A search program determined that sums of 149, 331, 373, 509, 701, 757,... allow A to make the statement that B cannot possibly know his number. B sees 1890 on A and determines he may have 2+945 (= 883+64), 5+378 (= 379+4), 7+270 (= 269+8), 10+189 (= 197+2), 14+135, 27+70 (= 89+8) or 35+54 (= 73 +16). Six of the possibilities are eliminated because the sum can be expressed as a prime plus a power of 2. This allows B to determine that 149 must be on his hat.

70

Three Logicians

Cases with certain proportions of the numbers on A:B:C are successively eliminated by the logicians' statements:
A1: Eliminates 2:1:1.

B1: Eliminates 1:2:1 and 2:3:1.

C1: Eliminates 1:1:2, 1:2:3, 2:1:3, 2:3:5. A2: 3:2:1, 4:3:1, 3:1:2, 5:2:3, 4:1:3, 8:3:5.

B2: Eliminates 1:3:2, 1:4:3, 2:5:3, 2:7:5, 3:4:1, 4:5:1, 3:5:2, 5:8:3, 4:7:3, 8:13:5.

C2: Deduces one of the proportions 3:2:5, 4:3:7, 3:1:4, 5:2:7, 4:1:5, 8:3:11, 1:3:4, 1:4:5, 2:5:7, 2:7:9, 3:4:7, 4:5:9, 3:5:8, 5:8:13, 4:7:11, 8:13:21.

Thus there are 16 possibilities for the numbers on A and B corresponding to the proportions above. (A, B) = (216216, 144144), (205920, 154440), (270270, 90090), (257400, 102960), (288288, 72072), (262080, 98280), (90090, 270270), (72072, 288288), (102960, 257400), (80080, 280280), (154440, 205920), (160160, 200200), (135135, 225225), (138600, 221760), (131040, 229320) and (137280, 223080).

71

Blind Logic

We can list all the possibilities of ABC as 100, 010, 001, 112, 121, 211, 144, 414, 441, 169, 196, 619, 691, 916, 961, 225, 252, 522, 256, 265, 526, 562, 625, 652, 289, 298, 829, 892, 928, 982, 234, 243, 324, 342, 423, 432, 136, 163, 316, 361, 613, 631, 004, 040, 400, 448, 484, 844, 259, 295, 529, 592, 925, 952, 567, 576, 657, 675, 756, 765, 667, 676, 766, 279, 297, 729, 792, 927, 972, 478, 487, 748, 784, 847, 874, 148, 184, 418, 481, 814, 841, 009, 090 and 900. A or C will know their number immediately except for the remaining cases: 414, 144, 441, 252, 256, 652, 448, 844, 484, 529, 852, 567, 765, 676, 148 and 841. Knowing only these remain, A and C will next reduce the set of possibilities to 144, 441, 252, 448, 844, 148 and 841. When no one makes an announcement A and C can further reduce the possibilities to 144, 441, 448, 844, 148 and 841. All of these remaining cases place a 4 on B and he so announces his number is a 4. There are six possible combinations for A and C.

72

Bell Ringer

List all possible doubles for the numbers on A and B, with the smaller number listed first: (0,6), (1,5), (2,4), (3,3), (0,11), (1,10), (2,9), (3,8), (4,7), (5,6), (0,19), (1,18), (2,17), (3,16), (4,15), (5,14), (6,13), (7,12), (8,11), (9,10). Before the bell rings the first time someone would immediately know his number if a number larger that 11 was used. This leaves cases (0,6), (1,5), (2,4), (3,3), (0,11), (1,10), (2,9), (3,8), (4,7), (5,6), (8,11), and (9,10). After the first bell the case (4,7) can be eliminated because the person seeing 7 would not hear the other announce the (7,12) case immediately. After the second bell (2,4) is eliminated. Successive bells eliminate (2,9), (9,10), (1,10), (1,5), (5,6), (0,6), (0,11), and (8,11) (after the tenth bell). This leaves cases (3,8) and (3,3). A sees 8 and B sees 3. A knows he must have a 3 on his hat but B is uncertain between 3 and 8 on his hat.

73

Counterfeit Stack?

Take one coin from stack A, four coins from stack B and five coins from stack C and weigh the ten coins in a group. If there is no counterfeit stack the weight will be 200 gm. For weights of 199, 198 or 197 gm stack A has fakes of weights 19, 18 or 17 gm, respectively. For weights of 196, 192 or 188 gm stack B has fakes of weights 19, 18 or 17 gm, respectively. For weights of 195, 190 or 185 gm stack C has fakes of weights 19, 18 or 17 gm, respectively.

74

Counterfeit Stacks 1

Gather 3, 6, 11, 12 and 13 coins respectively from stacks A, B, C, D and E and weigh the 45 coins in a group. If there is no counterfeit stack the weight will be 450 gm. The table shows which stacks are counterfeit depending on the total weight of the 45 coins.

Weight	Fakes	Weight	Fakes	Weight	Fakes
450	none	434	AE	428	ABE
447	A	433	BC	424	ACD
444	B	432	BD	423	ACE
439	C	431	BE	422	ADE
438	D	427	CD	421	BCD
437	E	426	CE	420	BCE
441	AB	425	DE	419	BDE
436	AC	430	ABC	414	CDE
435	AD	429	ABD		

75

Counterfeit Stacks 2

Take two coins from stack A and one from B and weigh them against two coins from stack D. This uses only five coins. The weight difference will be 7, 8, 9, 10, 11 or 12 gm, respectively, if A and B, A and C, B and C, A and D, B and D, or C and D are the stacks containing 9 gm coins.

76

Counterfeit Stacks 3

Label the stacks A to Q. There are 17 doublets, (a, b) with entries -3 to +3 having unique signed proportions a:b. Uniquely associate each stack with a doublet such as the following. A with (0, 0), B with (3, 0), C with (0, 3), D with (2, 2), E with (3, -3), F with (2, 1), G with (2, -1), H with (1,2), I with (1,-2), J with (3,1), K with (3, -1), L with (1, 3), M with (-1, 3), N with (3, 2), O with (3, -2), P with (2, 3), and Q with (2,-3). The doublet associated with a stack indicates which pan (+ for left pan and - for right pan) and how many coins from that stack are involved in each weighing. Thus the two weighings implied are 3B+2D+3E+2F+2G+H+I+3J+3K+L+3N+3O+2P+2Q versus M for the first weighing and 3C+2D+F+2H+J+3L+3M+2N+3P versus 3E+G+2I+K+2O+3Q for the second weighing. If all coins were true in the two weighings then the readings would be $W_1 = 30T$ and $W_2 = 8T$, where T is the weight of a true coin. Compute the following discriminators; $r_A = W_1 \div 30$ and $W_2 \div 8$, $r_B = W_2 \div 8$, $r_C = W_1 \div 30$, $r_D = (W_1 - W_2) \div 22$, $r_D = (W_1 - W_2) \div 22$, $r_E = (W_1 + W_2) \div 38$, $r_F = (W_1 - 2W_2) \div 14$, $r_G = (W_1 + 2W_2) \div 46$, $r_H = (2W_1 - W_2) \div 52$, $r_I = (2W_1 + W_2) \div 68$, $r_J = (W_1 - 3W_2) \div 6$, $r_K = (W_1 + 3W_2) \div 54$, $r_L = (3W_1 - W_2) \div 82$, $r_M = (3W_1 + W_2) \div 98$, $r_N = (2W_1 - 3W_2) \div 36$, $r_O = (2W_1 + 3W_2) \div 84$, $r_P = (3W_1 - 2W_2) \div 74$, $r_Q = (3W_1 + 2W_2) \div 106$. The discriminator for a stack is designed so that if that stack is fake its discriminator(s) will equal T, which is an integer. If both r_B and $r_C = T$ then A is the fake stack. The restriction that the weight of a fake coin differs from that of a true coin by less than 6 gm guarantees us that except for r_B and r_C no two discriminators can both be integers.

77

Compound Roots

If $x = (2+10/\sqrt{27})^{1/3} + (2-10/\sqrt{27})^{1/3}$, then $x^3 = 2+10/\sqrt{27} + 3(2+10/\sqrt{27})^{2/3}(2-10/\sqrt{27})^{1/3} + 3(2+10/\sqrt{27})^{1/3}(2-10/\sqrt{27})^{2/3} + 2-10/\sqrt{27} = 4+3x(4-100/27)^{1/3} = 4-2x$. Thus $x^3+2x-4 = 0$. The only real root is $x = 2$.

78

Island Hopping

(a) **Three planes.** The best that can be done is a distance of 29/18. We must solve three separate problems: (1) p_1, p_2 and p_3 are on the home island and must send p_1 to the destination island. (2) p_2 and p_3 are on the home island and must send p_2 to the destination island, where p_1 is available to receive p_2. (3) p_3 is on the home island and flies toward the destination island to be received by p_1 and p_2.

Problem (1) can be analyzed generally by setting up a co-ordinate system where $x = 0$ at the home island. We start by sending p_1, p_2 and p_3 out to point x_1. p_3 tops off p_1 and p_2 with fuel at x_1 and returns home. p_1 and p_2 continue to x_2, where p_2 tops off p_1. p_1 continues to the destination island while p_2 returns to point x_3, where p_3 refuels p_2 for safe return home. The fuel constraint at x_1 requires $x_1 \leq \frac{1}{4}$ to allow safe return of p_3. The fuel constraint at x_2 requires $2-2(x_2-x_1) \geq 1+(x_2-x_3)$. The fuel constraint at x_3 requires $x_3 \leq 1/3$. There is also a timing constraint for p_2 and p_3 traveling from x_1 to x_3. p_2 travels $(x_2-x_1) + (x_2-x_3)$ while p_3 travels x_1+x_3, so we must have $(x_2-x_1) +

$(x_2-x_3) \geq x_1+x_3$. This constraint assures that p_3 can get from x_1 back to the home island, refueled there and out to x_3 in time to meet p_2 before it runs out of fuel. We pick x_1, x_2 and x_3 to obey all constraints and maximize x_2. This occurs for $x_1 = \frac{1}{4}$, $x_3 = \frac{1}{3}$ and $x_2 = \frac{11}{18}$. The farthest the destination island can be is then $\frac{29}{18} = 1.611111...$The figure shows a time vs. distance graph for each plane.

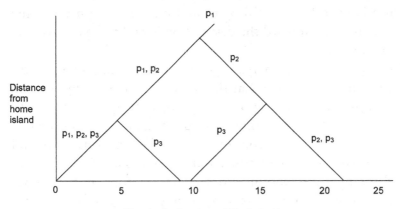

Time (unit = time to go 1/18 of a tank)

Problem (2) can be analyzed more easily. Send p_2 and p_3 out to $x = \frac{1}{3}$. p_3 tops off p_2 with fuel and returns home. p_2 continues to $x = \frac{4}{3}$, where p_1 refuels p_2 for safe passage to the destination island. This schedule allows the islands to be $\frac{5}{3}$ apart, which exceeds the maximum distance of problem (1).

Problem (3) can be analyzed by reversing the steps in problem (1). Send p_1 and p_2 out from the destination island a distance of $\frac{1}{3}$, where p_2 tops off p_1 and returns to the destination island. p_2 continues to a distance $\frac{11}{18}$ from the destination island where he is met by an empty p_3. p_2 and p_3 share the remaining $\frac{13}{18}$ of a tank from p_2 to get them to within $\frac{1}{4}$ of the destination island. At this point p_1 is available to share fuel to get them all safely to the destination island. The final result is that the farthest the destination island can be away is $^{29}/_{18}$ = 1.611111...

(b) **Four planes.** The best that can be done is a distance of $^{53}/_{30}$. We must solve four separate problems: (1) p_1, p_2, p_3 and p_4 are on the home island and must send p_1 to the destination island. (2) p_2, p_3, and p_4 are on the home island and must send p_2 to the destination island, where p_1 is available to receive p_2. (3) p_3 and p_4 are on the home island and must send p_3 to the destination island to be received by p_1 and p_2. (4) p_4 is on the home island and flies toward the destination island to be received by p_1, p_2 and p_3

Problem (1) can be analyzed generally by setting up a coordinate system where x = 0 at the home island. Start by sending p_1, p_2, p_3 and p_4 out to point x_1. p_4 tops off p_1, p_2 and p_3 with fuel at x_1 and returns home to refuel and go back out later to meet p_2. p_1, p_2 and p_3 continue to x_2, where p_3 tops off p_1 and p_2 and returns home to refuel and back out later to meet p_2 and p_4. p_1 and p_2 continue to x_3, where p_2 tops off p_1. p_1 continues on while p_2 returns to x_4, where p_4 shares fuel with p_2. p_2 and p_4 continue toward home to x_5, where p_3 receives them to share fuel to get them all home safely. The fuel constraint at x_1 requires $x_1 \leq 1/5$ to allow safe return of p_4. The fuel constraint at x_2 requires $3-3(x_2-x_1) \geq 2+x_2$. The fuel constraint at x_3 requires $2-2(x_3-x_2) \geq 1+(x_3-x_4)$. The fuel constraint at x_4 requires $1-x_4 \geq 2(x_4-x_5)$. The fuel constraint at x_5 requires $x_5 \leq 1/4$. There are also timing constraints. p_2 and p_4 travel from x_1 to x_4 with p_2 traveling $(x_3-x_1) + (x_3-x_4)$ while p_4 travels x_1+x_4, so we must have $(x_3-x_1) + (x_3-x_4) \geq x_1+x_4$. This constraint assures that p_4 can get from x_1 back to the home island, refuel there and out to x_4 in time to meet p_2 before it runs out of fuel. p_2 and p_3 travel from x_2 to x_5 with p_2 traveling $(x_3-x_2) + (x_3-x_5)$ while p_3 travels x_2+x_5, so we must have $(x_3-x_2) + (x_3-x_5) \geq x_2+x_5$. We pick x_1, to x_5 to obey all constraints and maximize x_3. This occurs for $x_1 = 1/5$, $x_5 = 1/4$, $x_4 = 1/2$, $x_2 = 2/5$ and $x_3 = ^{23}/_{30}$.

The farthest the destination island can be to get one aircraft to it is then $^{53}/_{30} = 1.766666\ldots$ The figure shows a time vs. distance graph for each plane.

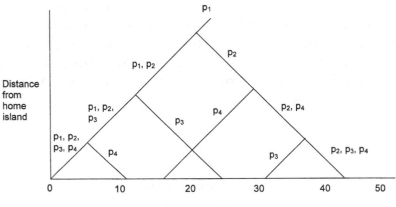

Time (unit = time to go 1/30 of a tank)

Problem (2) considers three planes on the home island and one plane on the destination island. This can be solved by noting that p_3 and p_4 can be used to send p_2 out as far as $^{29}/_{18}$ from the home island. p_1 can then come to it as far as $^{1}/_{3}$ from the destination island to share fuel and bring it home safely. The total gap can be as large as $^{35}/_{18}$, which is greater than $^{53}/_{30}$.

Problem (3) (two planes on each island) can be solved by noting that p_1 and p_2 can be used to receive p_3 as far out as $^{11}/_{18}$ from the destination island. With help from p_4, p_3 can be sent as far as $^{4}/_{3}$ from the home island. The total gap can be as large as $^{35}/_{18}$, which is greater than $^{53}/_{30}$.

Problem (4) (three planes on the destination island and one on the home island) can be analyzed by reversing the steps in problem (1). Send p_1, p_2 and p_3 out from the destination island a distance of $^{1}/_{4}$, where p_3 tops off p_1 and p_2 and returns to the destination island. p_1 and p_2 continue to a distance $^{1}/_{2}$

from the destination island where p_2 tops off p_1. p_1 continues on to meet p_4 and p_2 returns to the destination island. p_1 meets p_4 a unit distance from the home island and $23/30$ from the destination island, sharing $11/15$ tank of fuel with p_4. They get to within $2/5$ of the destination island and are met by p_3. p_3 shares his $3/5$ of a tank to get the three of them to within $1/5$ of the destination island. At this point p_2 is available to share fuel to get them all safely to the destination island. The final result is that the farthest the destination island can be away is $53/30 = 1.766666...$

79

Circumnavigation

(a) **Three planes.** The best that can be done is a circumference $C = 2$. This is analyzed generally by setting up a coordinate system where $x = 0$ at the home island. Start by sending p_1, p_2 and p_3 out to point x_1. p_3 tops off p_1 and p_2 with fuel at x_1 and returns home. p_1 and p_2 continue to x_2, where p_2 tops off p_1. p_1 continues around the planet. p_2 returns home, refuels and flies to x_3 in the reverse direction to meet p_1. They share fuel and fly to x_4, where p_3 meets them for a safe return home. The fuel constraint at x_1 requires $x_1 \le 1/4$ to allow a safe return of p_3. The fuel constraint at x_2 requires $2-2(x_2-x_1) \ge 1+x_2$. Getting p_1 from x_2 to x_3 requires $1 \ge C-x_2-x_3$. The fuel constraint at x_3 requires $1-x_3 \ge 2(x_3-x_4)$. The fuel constraint at x_4 requires $x_4 \le 1/4$. There is also a timing constraint for p_1 and p_2 traveling from x_2 to x_3. p_2 travels x_2+x_3 while p_1 travels $C-x_2-x_3$, so we must have $C-x_2-x_3 \ge x_2+x_3$. This constraint assures that p_2 can get from x_2 back to the home island, refueled there and out to x_3 in time to meet p_1 before it runs out of fuel. We pick x_1 to x_4 to obey all constraints and maximize C. There are multiple ways to do this but a symmetric one occurs for $x_1 = 1/4$, $x_2 =$

$x_3 = \frac{1}{2}$ and $x_4 = \frac{1}{4}$, giving C = 2. The figure shows a time vs. distance graph for each plane.

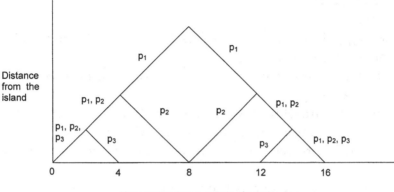

Time (unit = time to go 1/8 of a tank)

(b) Four planes. The best that I could do is a circumference C = $\frac{106}{45}$. Start by sending p_1, p_2, p_3 and p_4 out to point x_1. p_4 tops off p_1, p_2 and p_3 with fuel at x_1 and p_4 returns home to refuel and go back out later to meet p_2. p_1, p_2 and p_3 continue to x_2, where p_3 tops off p_1 and p_2 and returns home to refuel and go back out later to meet p_1. p_1 and p_2 continue to x_3, where p_2 tops off p_1. p_1 continues around the planet while p_2 returns to x_4, where p_4 shares fuel with p_2 to get them both safely home. From x_2, p_3 returns home, refuels and flies to x_5 toward the incoming p_1, share fuel with it and get both planes to x_6. Meanwhile p_2 and p_4 return home, refuel and fly toward p_1 to x_7. At x_7 p_4 tops off p_2 and returns home safely. p_2 continues on to meet p_1 and p_3 at x_6. p_1, p_2 and p_3 continue toward home to x_8 where they are met by p_4 to share fuel and return all planes safely home. There are fuel constraints at each of the transfer points.

At x_1: $x_1 \leq \frac{1}{5}$

At x_2: $3 - 3(x_2 - x_1) \geq 2 + x_2$

At x_3: $2-2(x_3-x_2) \geq 1+(x_3-x_4)$
At x_4: $1-x_4 \geq 2x_4$
At x_5: $1-x_5 \geq 2(x_5-x_6)$
At x_6: $1-(x_6-x_7) \geq 3(x_6-x_8)$
At x_7: $2-2x_7 \geq 1+x_7$
At x_8: $x_8 \leq \frac{1}{5}$

Getting p_1 from x_3 to x_5 requires $1 \geq C-x_3-x_5$. There are also timing constraints.

p_2 and p_4 travel from x_1 to x_4 so we must have (x_3-x_1) + $(x_3-x_4) \geq x_1+x_4$.

p_1 and p_3 travel from x_2 to x_5 so that $C-x_2-x_5 \geq x_2+x_5$.

p_1 and p_2 travel from x_3 to x_6 so that $C-x_3-x_6 \geq x_3+x_6$.

p_2 and p_4 travel from x_7 to x_8 so that (x_6-x_7) + $(x_6-x_8) \geq$ x_7+x_8.

We pick x_1 to x_8 to obey all constraints and maximize C. There are multiple ways to do this and one occurs for $x_1 = \frac{1}{5}$, $x_2 = \frac{2}{5}$, $x_3 = \frac{32}{45}$, $x_4 = \frac{1}{3}$, $x_5 = \frac{29}{45}$, $x_6 = \frac{7}{15}$, $x_7 = \frac{4}{15}$, $x_8 = \frac{1}{5}$ and C = $\frac{106}{45} = 2.355555....$ The figure shows a time vs. distance graph for each plane.

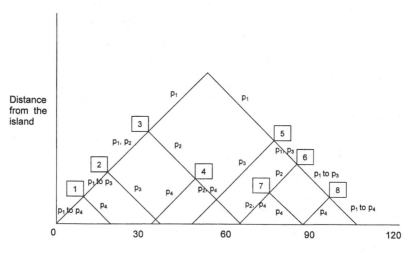

Time (unit = time to go 1/45 of a tank)

80

Colored Points

Color the two ends of all diameters with different colors. Since the hypotenuse of any inscribed right triangle is always a diameter, those two vertices will be different colors.

81

Chessboard Coloring

Yes. Turn the chessboard so that the upper left corner is black. Repaint the even columns and then repaint the even rows. The result is a black chessboard in 12 operations.

82

House Numbers

It is known that the sum of the first n fourth powers is $(3n^2+3n+1)/5$ times the sum of the first n squares. This leads to the equation $3n^2+3n+1=5m^2$, and possible solutions n = 1, 6, 86, 401, 5361, 24886,...

83

Integer Solutions

The equation can be rewritten as $y = 2x^2+5x+6+105/(2x-5)$. By letting 2x-5 take on all the factors of 105 we get 16 possible solutions: (x, y)=(-50, 4755), (-15, 378), (-8, 89), (-5, 24), (-1, -12), (0, -15), (1, -22), (2, -81), (3, 144), (4, 93), (5, 102), (6, 123), (10, 263), (13, 414), (20, 909), (55, 6332).

84

Test Results

$[(n-2)/n+(n-4)/n+(n-6)/n+a/n]/4 = \frac{3}{4}$ implies $a = 12$.

85

Palindrome Clock 1

The time was 12:55:21 when I woke up and 1:00:01 at the next palindrome time for a difference of 280 sec. The prior day I awoke at something like 6:49:46 and waited until 6:50:56 for the next palindrome time, a difference of 70 sec.

86

Palindrome Clock 2

The time was 4:01:04 pm on Dec 31, 2008. The three palindrome times were 3:59:53, 4:00:04 and 4:01:04. At 3:59:60 a leap second was added on Dec 31, 2008 so the interval was 12 seconds between the first two palindrome times. The prior leap second was inserted on Dec 31, 2005.

87

Special Numbers

The number of letters in the English name of the number divides evenly into the number. (a) 81, 100, 3136. (b) 39304. (c) 551, 1147.

88

Orthogonal Integer Medians

(a) The triangle with sides (26, 38, 44) has medians of lengths 24 and 39.

(b) Unknown.

89

Trilateration Problem

From the figure PA = 1, giving $x^2+y^2 = 1$. $PB^2 = 4$, leading to $s^2-2sx = 3$. $PC^2 = 9$ so $s^2+2yscos60-sx = 8$. Solving for s gives $s^2 = 7$, $x^2 = 4/7$ and $y^2 = 3/7$.

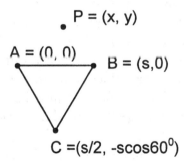

90

Two Triangles

A quick numerical check gives $(x, y, u, v) = (15,8,15,13)$. A computer search showed the next primitive solution to be $(x, y, u, v) = (8109409, 10130640, 12976609, 9286489)$.

91

Three Integer Triangles

a, b, and c are integers only if $\cos\theta = p/q$, where p and q are relatively prime integers. In (a) it follows that $15\theta < 180°$ or $\theta < 12°$. Thus $\cos\theta > .98714...$ and we get $q > 45$. Though this problem can be solved with algebra it is simpler to do it numerically. Pick $\cos\theta = 45/46$ and solve the four triangles independently. a = 529k, b = 1035k, c = 1496k; d = 418642136m, e = 529447005m, f = 709644761m; g = 172726942962199n, h = 189783039512880n, i = 1492523768123511n; c = 9105077114209855544177765r, f = 9112890370607127009948621r, i = 74941495473682687413031r.

k, m, n and r must be chosen so that both expressions for c, f and i agree. This gives i=11874523891390226215025012443486878974223987949968 from which the remaining lengths can be determined. Different values of $q > 45$ must be tried to see if common factors can be cancelled out producing even smaller i. In general even values of q allow a common factor of 64 to be removed; other factors must be searched for numerically. A search up to q=400 found no improvement to the above result.

In (b) it follows that $15\theta < 90°$ or $\theta < 6°$. Thus $\cos\theta > .99452...$ and we get $q > 182$. Though q=184 looks like a natural approach it turns out that q = 192 produces a common removable factor of 71 and gives the best result known. $\cos\theta = 191/192$ gives a = 9216k, b = 18336k, c = 27265k; d = 2315743395840m, e = 3050002612224m, f = 5033291921281m; g = 3263657262239977773576521n, h = 3840636646541084115902588n, i = 602100418462702407496537n; c = 594897197464884268007313490753509r,

f = 66167250529090574733887764689781 7r,
i = 906954042919390298566355588266574r. Thus
i = 150784063433011623421741956789701086887309120
593342113502985192202682110
from which the remaining lengths can be computed.

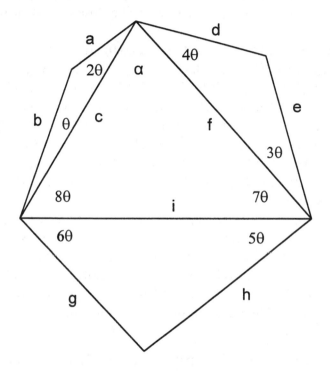

92

You're the Doctor

Notation: (A, B, fA, fB) indicates A ml and fA of a tablet in the larger vial and B ml and fB of a tablet in the smaller vial. The first step always begins by filling one or other vial and proceeds in sequence after each step. Putting in the tablet counts as a step.

Capacities of 5 ml and 3 ml.

(a) fraction = 10% (12 steps): (5,0,0,0), (2,3,0,0), (2,0,0,0), (0,2,0,0), (5,2,0,0), (4,3,0,0), (4,0,0,0), (4,0,1,0), (1,3,.25,.75), (1,0,.25,0), (5,0,.25,0), (2,3,.1,.15). The dose is now in the 5 ml vial.

(b) fraction = 13% (14 steps): (0,3,0,0), (0,3,0,1), (3,0,1,0), (3,3,0,1), (5,1,2/3,1/3), (3,3,.4,.6), (5,1,.8,.2), (3,3,.48,.52), (5,1,62/75,13/75), (0,1,0,13/75), (1,0,13/75,0), (1,3,13/75,0), (4,0,13/75,0), (1,3,13/300,.13). The dose is now in the 3 ml vial.

(c) fraction = 1% (18 steps): (0,3,0,0), (3,0,0,1), (3,3,0,0), (5,1,0,0), (5,1,1,0), (3,3,.6,.4), (5,1,13/15,2/15), (3,3,.52,.48), (5,1,.84,.16), (0,1,0,.16), (1,0,.16,0), (1,3,.16,0), (4,0,.16,0), (1,3,.04,.12), (1,0,.04,0), (1,3,.04,0), (4,0,.04,0), (1,3,.01,.03). The dose is now in the 5 ml vial.

(d) fraction = 7% (20 steps): (0,3,0,0), (3,0,0,0), (3,3,0,0), (3,3,0,1), (5,1,2/3,1/3), (0,1,0,1/3), (1,0,1/3,0), (1,3,1/3,0), (4,0,1/3,0), (1,3,1/12,.25), (1,0,1/12,0), (0,1,0,1/12), (0,3,0,1/12), (3,0,1/12,0), (3,3,1/12,0), (5,1,1/12,0), (3,3,.05,1/30), (5,1,13/180,1/90), (3,3,13/300,.04), (5,1,.07,1/75). The dose is now in the 5 ml vial.

Capacities of 5 ml and 4 ml.

(a) fraction = 50% (9 steps): (0,4,0,0), (4,0,0,0), (4,4,0,0), (5,3,0,0), (0,3,0,0), (3,0,0,0), (3,4,0,0), (3,4,0,1), (5,2,.5,.5). The dose is now in each vial.

(b) fraction = 61% (12 steps): (0,4,0,0), (4,0,0,0), (4,4,0,0), (5,3,0,0), (0,3,0,0), (3,0,0,0), (3,4,0,0), (3,4,0,1), (5,2,.5,.5), (3,4,.3,.7), (5,2,.65,.35), (3,4,.39,.61). The dose is now in the 4 ml vial.

(c) fraction = 74% (13 steps): (0,4,0,0), (4,0,0,0), (4,4,0,0), (5,3,0,0), (0,3,0,0), (3,0,0,0), (3,4,0,0), (5,2,0,0), (5,2,1,0), (3,4,.6,.4), (5,2,.8,.2), (3,4,.48,.52), (5,2,.74,.26). The dose is now in the 5 ml vial.

(d) fraction = 38% (18 steps): (0,4,0,0), (4,0,0,0), (4,4,0,0), (5,3,0,0), (0,3,0,0), (3,0,0,0), (3,4,0,0), (3,4,0,1), (5,2,.5,.5), (0,2,0,.5), (0,4,0,.5), (4,0,.5,0), (4,4,.5,0), (5,3,.5,0), (4,4,.4,.1), (5,3,.425,.075), (4,4,.34,.16), (5,3,.38,.12). The dose is now in the 5 ml vial.

Capacities of 10 ml and 7 ml.

(a) fraction = 40% (7 steps): (0,7,0,0), (7,0,0,0), (7,7,0,0), (7,7,0,1), (10,4,3/7,4/7), (7,7,.3,.7), (10,4,.6,.4). The dose is now in the 7 ml vial.

(b) fraction = 10% (11 steps): (10,0,0,0), (3,7,0,0), (3,0,0,0), (0,3,0,0), (10,3,0,0), (6,7,0,0), (6,0,0,0), (0,6,0,0), (10,6,0,0), (10,6,1,0), (9,7,.9,.1). The dose is now in the 7 ml vial.

(c) fraction = 50% (17 steps): (10,0,0,0), (3,7,0,0), (3,0,0,0), (0,3,0,0), (10,3,0,0), (6,7,0,0), (6,0,0,0), (0,6,0,0), (10,6,0,0), (9,7,0,0), (9,0,0,0), (2,7,0,0), (2,0,0,0), (0,2,0,0), (10,2,0,0), (10,2,1,0), (5,7,.5,.5). The dose is now in each vial.

(d) fraction = 25% (21 steps): (10,0,0,0), (3,7,0,0), (3,0,0,0), (0,3,0,0), (10,3,0,0), (6,7,0,0), (6,0,0,0), (0,6,0,0), (10,6,0,0), (9,7,0,0), (9,0,0,0), (2,7,0,0), (2,0,0,0), (0,2,0,0), (10,2,0,0), (10,2,1,0), (5,7,.5,.5), (5,0,.5,0), (5,7,.5,0), (10,2,.5,0), (5,7,.25,.25). The dose is now in each vial.

(e) fraction = 29% (24 steps): (10,0,0,0), (3,7,0,0), (3,0,0,0), (0,3,0,0), (10,3,0,0), (6,7,0,0), (6,0,0,0), (0,6,0,0), (10,6,0,0), (9,7,0,0), (9,0,0,0), (2,7,0,0), (2,0,0,0), (0,2,0,0), (10,2,0,0), (10,2,1,0), (5,7,.5,.5), (0,7,0,.5), (7,0,.5,0), (7,7,.5,0), (10,4,.5,0), (7,7,.35,.15), (10,4,29/70,3/35), (7,7,.29,.21). The dose is now in the 10 ml vial.

(f) fraction = 19% (29 steps): (10,0,0,0), (3,7,0,0), (3,0,0,0), (0,3,0,0), (10,3,0,0), (6,7,0,0), (6,0,0,0), (0,6,0,0), (10,6,0,0), (9,7,0,0), (9,0,0,0), (2,7,0,0), (2,0,0,0), (0,2,0,0), (10,2,0,0), (10,2,1,0), (5,7,.5,.5), (5,0,.5,0), (5,7,.5,0), (10,2,.5,0), (5,7,.25,.25), (0,7,0,.25), (7,0,.25,0), (7,7,.25,0), (10,4,.25,0), (7,7,.175,.075), (10,4,29/140,3/70), (7,7,.145,.105), (10,4,.19,.06). The dose is now in the 10 ml vial.

Capacities of 10 ml and 9 ml.

(a) fraction = 30% (11 steps): (10,0,0,0), (1,9,0,0), (1,0,0,0), (0,1,0,0), (10,1,0,0), (2,9,0,0), (2,0,0,0), (0,2,0,0), (10,2,0,0), (10,2,1,0), (3,9,.3,.7). The dose is now in the 10 ml vial.

(b) fraction = 40% (15 steps): (10,0,0,0), (1,9,0,0), (1,0,0,0), (0,1,0,0), (10,1,0,0), (2,9,0,0), (2,0,0,0), (0,2,0,0), (10,2,0,0), (3,9,0,0), (3,0,0,0), (0,3,0,0), (10,3,0,0), (10,3,1,0), (4,9,.4,.6). The dose is now in the 10 ml vial.

(c) fraction = 50% (19 steps): (10,0,0,0), (1,9,0,0), (1,0,0,0), (0,1,0,0), (10,1,0,0), (2,9,0,0), (2,0,0,0), (0,2,0,0), (10,2,0,0), (3,9,0,0), (3,0,0,0), (0,3,0,0), (10,3,0,0), (4,9,0,0), (4,0,0,0), (0,4,0,0), (10,4,0,0), (10,4,1,0), (5,9,.5,.5). The dose is now in each vial.

(d) fraction = 5% (22 steps): (10,0,0,0), (1,9,0,0), (1,0,0,0), (0,1,0,0), (10,1,0,0), (2,9,0,0), (2,0,0,0), (0,2,0,0), (10,2,0,0), (3,9,0,0), (3,0,0,0), (0,3,0,0), (10,3,0,0), (4,9,0,0), (4,0,0,0), (0,4,0,0), (10,4,0,0), (10,4,1,0), (5,9,.5,.5), (5,0,.5,0), (10,0,.5,0), (1,9,.05,.45). The dose is now in the 10 ml vial.

(e) fraction = 41% (26 steps): (10,0,0,0), (1,9,0,0), (1,0,0,0), (0,1,0,0), (10,1,0,0), (2,9,0,0), (2,0,0,0), (0,2,0,0), (10,2,0,0), (3,9,0,0), (3,0,0,0), (0,3,0,0), (10,3,0,0), (4,9,0,0), (4,0,0,0), (0,4,0,0), (10,4,0,0), (10,4,1,0), (5,9,.5,.5), (0,9,0,.5), (9,0,.5,0), (9,9,.5,0), (10,8,.5,0), (9,9,.45,.05), (10,8,41/90,2/45), (9,9,.41,.09). The dose is now in the 10 ml vial.

(f) fraction = 57% (27 steps): (0,9,0,0), (9,0,0,0), (9,9,0,0), (10,8,0,0), (0,8,0,0), (8,0,0,0), (8,9,0,0), (10,7,0,0), (0,7,0,0), (7,0,0,0), (7,9,0,0), (10,6,0,0), (0,6,0,0), (6,0,0,0), (6,0,1,0), (6,9,1,0), (10,5,1,0), (6,9,.6,.4), (10,5,7/9,2/9), (6,9,7/15,8/15), (10,5,.19/27,8/27), (10,0,.19/27,0), (1,9,19/270,19/30), (0,9,0,19/30), (9,0,19/30,0), (10,0,19/30,0), (1,9,19/300,.57). The dose is now in the 9 ml vial.

(g) fraction = 33% (27 steps): (0,9,0,0), (9,0,0,0), (9,9,0,0), (10,8,0,0), (0,8,0,0), (8,0,0,0), (8,9,0,0), (10,7,0,0), (0,7,0,0), (7,0,0,0), (7,9,0,0), (10,6,0,0), (0,6,0,0), (6,0,0,0), (6,9,0,0),

(6,9,0,1), (10,5,4/9,5/9), (6,9,4/15,11/15), (10,5,16/27,11/27),
(0,5,0,11/27), (5,0,11/27,0), (10,0,11/27,0), (1,9,11/270,11/30),
(0,9,0,11/30), (9,0,11/30,0), (10,0,11/30,0), (1,9,11/300,.33).
The dose is now in the 9 ml vial.

93

AIDS Test

2%. If 1,000 people were tested, 50 would show positive and
one of those would actually have AIDS.

94

Random Chords

The probability of intersection is one third. Suppose all four
random points are chosen first. There are three ways to draw a
pair of chords through these four points and one way has them
intersecting inside the circle as shown in the figure.

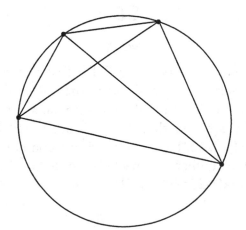

95

Cubic Triangles

The probability of an acute triangle is $\frac{1}{7}$; the probability of a right triangle is $\frac{6}{7}$ as seen from the list below.

Right = 123, 124, 125, 126, 127, 128, 134, 136, 138, 145, 146, 147, 148, 156, 158, 167, 168, 178.

Acute = 135, 137, 157

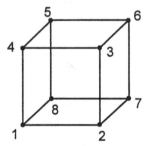

96

Typos

Let the total number of typos be T. The first reader finds typos with a probability 252/T and misses them with a probability (1-252/T). Probabilities for the second reader are 255/T and (1-255/T). We are told that 20 typos are found by both so 20/T = (252/T)×(255/T), from which we compute T = 3213 typos. Thus the number of expected typos to be missed by both is T×(1-252/T)×(1-255/T) = 2726.

97

Misplaced Averages

The three families could have had 8 children, 2 children and 2 children respectively. Thus the average family has $4 = (8+2+2)/3$ children but the average number of siblings for a child is $5 = (8×7+2×1+2×1)/12$.

98

The Roving Ant

For all parts of this problem it's useful to draw a map of the vertices and edges of the polyhedron. The vertex marked 0 is the starting point and the diametrically opposite vertex is marked d. Vertices marked n are n moves away from the starting vertex. Define E_n as the expected number of moves the fly must make from vertex n to reach vertex d.

(a) For the octahedron we get equations $E_0 - 1 + E_1$, $E_1 - 1 + E_0/4 + E_1/2$, which leads to $E_1 = 5$ and $E_0 = 6$. So the expected time is 6 minutes for the octahedron.

(b) For the cube we get equations $E_0 = 1 + E_1$, $E_1 = 1 + E_0/3 + 2E_2/3$, $E_2 = 1 + 2E_1/3$, which leads to $E_2 = 7$, $E_1 = 9$ and $E_0 = 10$. The expected time is 10 minutes for the cube.

(c) For the dodecahedron we get equations $E_0 = 1 + E_1$, $E_1 = 1 + E_0/3 + 2E_2/3$, $E_2 = 1 + E_1/3 + E_2/3 + E_3/3$, $E_3 = 1 + E_2/3 + E_3/3 + E_4/3$, $E_4 = 1 + 2E_3/3$, which leads to $E_4 = 19$, $E_3 = 27$, $E_2 = 32$, $E_1 = 34$, and $E_0 = 35$. The expected time is 35 minutes for the dodecahedron.

(d) For the icosahedron we get equations $E_0 = 1 + E_1$, $E_1 = 1 + E_0/5 + 2E_1/5 + 2E_2/5$, $E_2 = 1 + 2E_1/5 + 2E_2/5$, which leads to

$E_2 = 11$, $E_1 = 14$, and $E_0 = 15$. So the expected time is 15 minutes for the icosahedron.

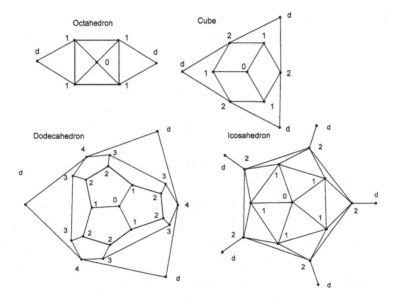

99

Random Toss

The probability that the disk lands on one tile only is $P = (1-d)^2$ and the probability it covers a corner is $P_D = \pi d^2/4$ so the probability of winning is $P = 1-P_C-P_D$. This function is maximized for $d = 4/(\pi+4) \approx .560099153...$Interestingly this gives a maximum win probability of $P = 4/(\pi+4) \approx .560099153...$

100

Tuesday's Child

Imagine a perfectly representative collection of 196 families with two children. 49 will have two boys (BB), 49 will have two girls (GG) and the remaining 98 will be a boy and a girl in some birth order (BG or GB). The second statement reduces the collection to 147 families that include at least one boy. The third statement reduces the BG and GB sets from 49 families to 7 families each and reduces the BB set to 13 families (12 families where exactly one boy is born on Tuesday and one family where both are born on Tuesday). Of the 27 families satisfying all three statements 13 of them have two boys so the probability of two boys is 13/27.

101

Monkeys and Typewriters

The giant string of characters will have $n = 3.1556952 \times 10^{34}$ characters. This follows from 1 year = 3.1556952×10^7 seconds (Gregorian calendar used). From this string there are $n-17$ opportunities to hit the exact 18 that produce the desired quote. For any one of these the probability of making a hit is $p = 100^{-18} = 10^{-36}$. The probability of missing on all $n-17$ opportunities is $Q = (1-p)^{n-17}$. The natural logarithm of Q is $\ln Q = (n-17) \times \ln(1-p) \approx -np$, so that $Q \approx e^{-np} = .968936$. The probability that the quote will be there is $1-Q = .03106423...$, or slightly more than 3%.

102

The Bible in Pi

A string of n digits of pi will provide $n-m+1$ opportunities for a group of m digits to match in consecutive order. For any one of these the probability of making a hit is $p = 10^{-m}$. The probability of missing on all $n-m+1$ opportunities is $Q = (1-p)^{n-m+1}$. The natural logarithm of Q is $\ln Q = (n-m+1)\ln(1-p) \approx -np$, so that $Q \approx e^{-np}$. If we set $Q \approx .5$ then $n \approx .693147/p = .693147 \times 10^m$.

For our case m = 8680450, so n ≈ $6.93147 \times 10^{8680449}$. Thus the complete Bible is encoded in the decimal expansion of pi every $6.93147 \times 10^{8680449}$ digits or so.

103

Find Dick Hess in Pi

The name, Dick Hess, has nine 2-digit blocks. The first eight blocks must be different and because of the SS in Hess the 9th must match the 8th. With random digits the probability of this for nine consecutive blocks is p = (100/100)×(99/100) ×(98/100)×(97/100)×(96/100)×(95/100)×(94/100)×(93/100)× (1/100). One divided by p is 137.279 so we expect we may have to examine about 137 digits of pi to get the name, Dick Hess. In actual fact we must go to digits 399 to 416, which read 943305727036575959. Thus D=94, I=33, C=05, K=72, blank=70, H=36, E=57 and S=59 does the job.

104

Make 29–Intermediate Rules

a. $29 = 9 \div .3 - 1$

b. $29 = 2^5 - 3$

c. $29 = (6-.2) \div .2$

d. $29 = (9-.3) \div .3$

e. $29 = 58 \times .5$

f. $29 = 7 \div .2 - 6 = 6^2 - 7$

g. $29 = 3 \div .1 - 1 = (3-.1) \div .1$

h. $29 = .5^{-5} - 3$

i. $29 = .2^{-2} + 4$

105

Puzzles with Consecutive Scoring Numbers

a. $21 = 2 \div \underline{.1} + 3 = (2 + \underline{.3}) \div \underline{.1}$

b. $35 = 3 + {}^{.1}\sqrt{\sqrt{2}} = (3! + 1) \div .2 = 3!^2 - 1$

c. $45 = (2 + 3) \div \underline{.1} = 3 \div (.2 \times \sqrt{.1}) = 3! \div (\sqrt{.1} - .2)$

d. $56 = 3! \div \underline{.1} + 2 = ({}^{\sqrt{.1}}\sqrt{2})! \div 3!! = (3! + \underline{.2}) / \underline{.1}$

e. $56 = (2 + \underline{.3}) \times 4! = \sqrt{(3!! \div .2)} - 4 = (2 \times 4)! / 3!! = (\sqrt{\sqrt{\sqrt{2^{4!}}}})! \div 3!! = 32 + 4!$

f. $70 = 3! + \sqrt{\sqrt{2^{4!}}} = 3 \times 4! - 2 = 4! \div \underline{.3} - 2$

g. $38 = 3!^2 + \sqrt{4} = \sqrt{(2 \times 3!! + 4)} = 2 + (3!)^{\sqrt{4}} = 2 + \sqrt{(3!)^4} = \sqrt{[2 \times (3!! + \sqrt{4})]} = 3! + {}^{.2}\sqrt{\sqrt{4}} = \sqrt{[\sqrt{4} \times (3!! + 2)]}$

h. $95 = 3!! - 5^4$

i. $67 = 3 \times 4! - 5 = 4! \div \underline{.3} - 5 = 3 + \sqrt{\sqrt{.5^{-4!}}}$

j. $52 = (5! - 3) \times \underline{.4} = 5! \times .4\underline{3}$

k. $58 = 56 + \sqrt{4} = \sqrt{(5 \times 6!)} - \sqrt{4} = \sqrt{\sqrt{.5^{-4!}}} - 6$

l. $13 = 5 + 6 + \sqrt{4} = 4! - 5 - 6 = 5 + \sqrt{\sqrt{4^6}} = 5 + {}^{.6}\sqrt{4} = 6 \div \underline{.4} - .5 = 5 \times (\sqrt{4} + .6) = (4! - .6) \times \underline{.5} = (6 + .5) \times \sqrt{4}$

m. $45 = 6! \times .5^4 = 5! \div (4 \times \underline{.6}) = 6 \times 5 \div \sqrt{.4} = 5! \div (\sqrt{4} + \underline{.6}) = 4! \div .6 + 5 = \sqrt{4} \div (.6 - \underline{.5}) = \sqrt{(6! \times \underline{.5})} \div \underline{.4}$

n. $9 = {}^{-.5}\sqrt{\sqrt{(.\underline{7} - \underline{.6})}} = \sqrt{(75 + 6)}$

o. $11 = \sqrt{(5! + 7 - 6)} = 7 \div \underline{.6} + .5$

p. $94 = 5! \times .\underline{7} + \underline{.6}$

q. $40 = 7! \div (5! + 6) = 5! \times \sqrt{(.\underline{7} - \underline{.6})}$

r. $60 = \sqrt{(7! - 6! \div .5)} = 6! \div (5 + 7) = \sqrt{[6! \div (.7 - .5)]} = \sqrt{[5! \div (.7 - \underline{.6})]}$

s. $10 = \sqrt{\sqrt{\sqrt{(.\underline{7} - .6)^{-8}}}} = (7 + 8) \times \underline{.6}$

t. $11 = 8^{.6} + 7$

u. $12 = 8! \div 7! \div \underline{.6} = \sqrt{[\sqrt{(8! \div .7)} \times .6]}$

v. $16 = 6! \times (.8 - .\underline{7})$

w. $39 = 7 + {}^{.6}\sqrt{8}$

x. $11 = 8! \div 7! + \sqrt{9} = (9 + .\underline{7}) \div \underline{.8}$

y. $67 = \sqrt{(7! \times .\underline{8} + 9)}$

z. $39 = \sqrt{(\sqrt{9^8} - 7!)}$

106

Make 75

a. $75 = 5! \div (.8 + .8)$

b. $75 = .6 \times \sqrt{5^6} = 5 \div (.\underline{6} - .6)$

c. $75 = \sqrt{(\cdot^2\sqrt{.2} \div .\underline{5})}$

d. $75 = 5! \div (0! + .6) = 5 \div .0\underline{6}$

e. $75 = 5 \times 15 = 5! - 5 \div .\underline{1} = 5 \times 5 \div \sqrt{.1} = \cdot^5\sqrt{5} \div \sqrt{.1} = \sqrt{[(\cdot^1\sqrt{\sqrt{5}}) \div .\underline{5}]}$

f. $75 = 25 \div \sqrt{.1} = 15 \div .2 = 5^2 \div \sqrt{.1} = 5 \div (.2 \times \sqrt{.1}) = \cdot^5\sqrt{.2} \div \sqrt{.1} = \sqrt{[(\cdot^1\sqrt{\sqrt{.2}}) \div .\underline{5}]}$

g. $75 = 3 \times \sqrt{\sqrt{5^8}} = \sqrt{\sqrt{5^8}} \div .\underline{3} = \sqrt{(3!! \times 5)} \div .8 = (3!! - 5!) \div 8$

h. $75 = \sqrt{(.2^{-4} \times 9)} = (\sqrt{9}) \div .2^{\sqrt{4}} = (\sqrt{9})! \div (.2 \times .4) = (4! - 9) \div .2$

107

Targets by 10s

a. $20 = 8^{\sqrt{.1}} \div .1$

b. $60 = (\sqrt{.2^{-2}})! \div 2 = \sqrt{\{[\sqrt{(2/.\underline{2})}]!!/.2\}}$

c. $70 = 8! \div (4!)^2 = 28 \div .4$

d. $100 = \sqrt{(.7 - .6)^4} = (.7 - .6)^{\sqrt{4}} = 76 + 4!$

e. $50 = 8 \div \sqrt{\sqrt{(.4^8)}}$

f. $30 = 0! \div (.7 - .\underline{6})$

g. $90 = 5! \div \sqrt{(2 - .\underline{2})}$

h. $100 = (3 + 7)^2 = 3!! \div (7 + .2)$

i. $70 = 35/.5 = (5! + 3!) \times .\underline{5}$

j. $80 = [\sqrt{(7 + 9)}]! \div .3 = (7 - \sqrt{9})! \div .3 = \sqrt{[(7! + 3!!) \div .9]}$

k. $30 = \sqrt{[7! \div (6 - .4)]} = (4! - .\underline{6}) \div .\underline{7} = 6 \times (7 - \sqrt{4}) = \sqrt{(.7 - .\underline{6})^{-\sqrt{4}}} = \sqrt{\sqrt{(.7 - .\underline{6})^{-4}}}$

l. $90 = 5! \times .75 = 5! \div (.\underline{5} + .\underline{7})$

m. $40 = (8^{-\underline{6}})! \div .6 = \sqrt{(6! \times .8)} \div .6$

n. $90 = 5! \div \sqrt{(.\underline{8} + .\underline{8})} = (8 - 5)!!/8$

o. $20 = [\sqrt{(8 + 0!)}]! \div .3 = \sqrt{[3!!/(0! + .8)]}$

p. $90 = 5! \div \sqrt{(0! + .\underline{7})}$

q. $50 = \sqrt{(.1^{-3} \div .4)} = \sqrt{[\sqrt{(.1^{-3!})} \div .4]} = 3! \div .\underline{1} - 4 = (\sqrt{4} + 3) \div .1 = (3! - .\underline{4}) \div .\underline{1} = \sqrt{[^{-.3}\sqrt{(.1)} / .4]}$

r. $100 = {}^{-.5}\sqrt{(.3 - .2)} = 5! \div (3! \times .2) = \sqrt{(5! \div .3)} \div .2 = \sqrt{(3!! \times .\underline{5})} \div .2$

s. $90 = (2 \times 5)! \div 8! = 5! \div \sqrt{(2 \times .\underline{8})} = (5 - 2)!!/8$

t. $90 = 3 \div (.7 - \sqrt{.\underline{4}})$

u. $90 = \sqrt{(7! \div .6\underline{2})}$

v. $60 = \sqrt{(7! \div (\sqrt{4} - .6))} = \sqrt{(7! - \sqrt{4} \times 6!)} = \sqrt{[(7 - \sqrt{4}) \times 6!]} = \sqrt{4} \div (.7 - .\underline{6})$

w. $70 = {}^{.5}\sqrt{(7!)} \div 9!$

x. $60 = \sqrt{[3!! \div (0! - .8)]}$

y. $30 = 7 \div (\sqrt{.\underline{1}} - .1)$

z. $90 = 7 \div (.3 - .\underline{2}) = 27 \div .3$

aa. $80 = 7! \div 63 = 3!! \times (.\underline{7} - .\underline{6})$

bb. $60 = \sqrt{[(7 - \sqrt{4}) \times \sqrt{9}!!]} = \sqrt{[7! \div (.4 + .\underline{9})]} = \sqrt{(7! - \sqrt{4} \times \sqrt{9}!!)} = [\sqrt{(7 + 9)}]! \div .4 = (7 - \sqrt{9})! \div .4$

cc. $100 = \sqrt{\sqrt{(4 + \sqrt{9}!)}^8} = \sqrt{(.9 - .8)^{-4}} = (.9 - .8)^{-\sqrt{4}} = 98 + \sqrt{4}$

dd. $50 = \sqrt{(.2^{-5} \times .8)} = \sqrt{(^{-2}\sqrt{5} \times .8)} = (2 + 8) \times 5 = \sqrt{\sqrt{(.2^{-8})}} \div .5 = 2 \times \sqrt{\sqrt{5^8}}$

ee. $0 = {}^{-\sqrt{.1}}\sqrt{.5} - 8 = .\underline{8} - .\underline{5} - \sqrt{.\underline{1}}$ (Each side can have a square root or factorial taken an arbitrary number of times)

ff. $100 = \sqrt{\sqrt{\sqrt{\sqrt{\sqrt{\sqrt{.1}}}}}}{}^u$, where $u = -\sqrt{4^7}$

108

Make 29–Expert Rules

a. $29 = (7 - .\underline{5}) \div .2$

b. $29 = (9 + .\underline{6}) \times \sqrt{9}$

c. $29 = 5 + 8 \div \sqrt{.1}$

d. $29 = 5 + [\sqrt{(8 + 8)}]!$

e. $29 = 7 \div .2 - (\sqrt{9})! = (\sqrt{9})!^2 - 7$

f. $29 = \sqrt{(7! \div \sqrt{9}! + 0!)}$

g. $29 = (.\underline{6} + 9) \div \sqrt{.1}$

h. $29 = 6 \div .\underline{2} + \sqrt{4} = (6 + .\underline{4}) \div .\underline{2}$

i. $29 = \sqrt{(3!! \div .8)} - 0!$

j. $29 = 6 \div .2 - .\underline{9} = 26 + \sqrt{9} = 2 + \sqrt{\sqrt{9^6}} = 2 + \sqrt{(6! + 9)}$

k. $29 = (6 \times .\underline{6})! + 5$

l. $29 = {}^{.\underline{6}}\sqrt{8} - 3$

m. $29 = \sqrt{(3!^4)} - 7 = 3!^{\sqrt{4}} - 7$

n. $29 = \sqrt{(7 \times 5! + 0!)}$

o. $29 = 2 + {}^{-\sqrt{.\underline{1}}}\sqrt{\sqrt{.\underline{1}}}$

p. $29 = \sqrt{(\sqrt{9}!! + 5! + 0!)} = (\sqrt{9} + 0!)!! + 5 = 5 \times \sqrt{9}! - 0!$

q. $29 = 5 \times 6 - .\underline{9} = 9 + \sqrt{(6! \times .\underline{5})} = 5! \div 6 + 9 = \sqrt{(5! + 6! + .\underline{9})} = (.\underline{6} \times \sqrt{9}!)! + 5$

r. $29 = 4 + \sqrt{\sqrt{.2^{-8}}} = 4! + \sqrt{\sqrt{\sqrt{.2^{-8}}}} = 4! \div .\underline{8} + 2$

s. $29 = 4! + 2 \div .4 = .2^{-\sqrt{4}} + 4 = 4 + \sqrt{.2^{-4}} = 4! + \sqrt{.2^{-\sqrt{4}}} = 4! + \sqrt{\sqrt{.2^{-4}}}$

t. $29 = (8^{.\underline{6}})! + 5 = \sqrt{(6! \times .8)} + 5$

u. $29 = \sqrt{\sqrt{\sqrt{(4! + 5)^8}}} = (8 - 4)! + 5 = [\sqrt{(8 \times \sqrt{4})}]! + 5 = (8^{\sqrt{.4}})! + 5 = (8 \div \sqrt{4})! + 5 = 5 + \sqrt{\sqrt{\sqrt{(4!)^8}}} = [\sqrt{(4! - 8)}]! + 5 = 4! + \sqrt{\sqrt{\sqrt{5^8}}} = 4 + \sqrt{\sqrt{5^8}} = 58 \div \sqrt{4}$

109

Head-Splitting MathDice Puzzles

a. $32 = {}^{.\underline{3}}\sqrt{\sqrt{(1+7)}} = {}^{.\underline{1}}\sqrt{\sqrt{\sqrt{(7-3)}}}$

b. $41 = \sqrt{(7! \times \sqrt{.\underline{1}} + 1)}$

c. $84 = \sqrt{({}^{.\underline{1}}\sqrt{\sqrt{(3!)}} - 3!!)}$

d. $43 = 5 \div .\underline{1} - \sqrt{4} = (4! - .\underline{1}) \div .\underline{5}$

e. $67 = 5! \times .\underline{5} + \sqrt{.\underline{1}}$

f. $16 = (\sqrt{16})! \times .\underline{6} = (6 - .\underline{6}) \div \sqrt{.\underline{1}}$

g. $16 = 6 \times \sqrt{(7 + .\underline{1})}$

h. $57 = \sqrt{[(3!! + 2) \div .\underline{2}]}$

i. $76 = \sqrt{[(3!! + 2) \times 8]} = 38 \times 2 = 82 - 3!$

j. $45 = 8 \div (.4 - .\underline{2}) = (8 + \sqrt{4}) \div \underline{2}$

k. $26 = (5 + .\underline{7}) \div .2$

l. $22 = 6 \div .\underline{27}$

m. $32 = (7 - .6) \div .2 = {}^{.7 \text{-}.6}\sqrt{\sqrt{2}}$

n. $23 = (6 - .\underline{8}) \div .\underline{2}$

o. $27 = \sqrt{(7 \div .\underline{7})!} \div .\underline{2}$

p. $66 = \sqrt{[(3!! + 3!) \times 3!]}$

q. $19 = \sqrt{[(5! + .\underline{3}) \times 3]} = (5! - 3!) \div 3! = \sqrt{[(5! + .\underline{3}) / .\underline{3}]}$

r. $23 = 7 \div .3 - .\underline{3}$

s. $27 = .\underline{1}^{-.7 \text{-}.8} = {}^{-\sqrt{.1}}\sqrt{\sqrt{(.\underline{8} - .\underline{7})}} = {}^{-\sqrt{(.\underline{8} \text{-}.\underline{7})}}\sqrt{\sqrt{.\underline{1}}}$

t. $95 = 38 \div .4$

u. $28 = .\underline{7} \times \sqrt{\sqrt{3!^8}} = \sqrt{(8! \times .7)} \div 3!$

v. $32 = {}^{.3}\sqrt{\sqrt{(9 - .\underline{9})}}$

w. $58 = \sqrt{(4 + 7! \times \sqrt{.\underline{4}})}$

x. $45 = 7 \div (.6 - .\underline{4})$

y. $87 = (6! - 4!) \div 8$

z. $84 = \sqrt{(7! \times .4 + 7!)} = (7 - \sqrt{4})! \times .7 = \sqrt{(7! \times .7 \times \sqrt{4})}$

aa. $47 = 47^{.2} = 47 \times .\underline{9} = 47 \div .\underline{9} = \sqrt{(7! + .\underline{9})} - 4!$

bb. $76 = 9! \div 7! + 4$

cc. $82 = \sqrt{[(8! + 4!) \div \sqrt{9!}]} = \sqrt{[4 + 8! \div \sqrt{9!}]}$

dd. $84 = 8! \div [(\sqrt{9})!! \times \sqrt{.\underline{4}}] = 84^{.2} = 84 \times .\underline{9} = 84 \div .\underline{9}$

ee. $66 = .55 \times 5!$

ff. $56 = [\sqrt{(.5^{-6})}]! \div 6!$

gg. $13 = \sqrt{(5! + 7 \times 7)}$

hh. $27 = \sqrt{\sqrt{(.\underline{7} - .\underline{6})^{-6}}} = {}^{-.6}\sqrt{(.\underline{7} - .\underline{6})}$

ii. $13 = (8 + .\underline{6}) \div .\underline{6}$

jj. $35 = .\underline{7} \div (.8 - .\underline{7})$

kk. $55 = \sqrt{(7! \times .6 + .\underline{9})}$

ll. $49 = \sqrt{[(3!! \div .3 + 0!]}$

mm. $31 = {}^{.3}\sqrt{\sqrt{8}} - 0! = 0! + \sqrt{(3!! \div .8)}$

nn. $41 = \sqrt{(8! \div 4! + 0!)}$

oo. $4 = (7+0!)^{-6} = (7-0!) \times \underline{.6}$

pp. $32 = {}^{0!-.7}\sqrt{\sqrt{8}}$

qq. $57 = {}^{-.5}\sqrt{.\underline{1}}-4! = (4!-5) \div \sqrt{.\underline{1}}$

rr. $92 = (.1+\sqrt{.\underline{4}}) \times 5!$

ss. $54 = 4! \div (.\underline{7}-\sqrt{.\underline{1}}) = (7-4)! \div .\underline{1} = [\sqrt{(7+\sqrt{4})}]! \div .\underline{1}$

tt. $68 = 5! \times (.9-\sqrt{.\underline{1}})$

uu. $32 = {}^{.1}\sqrt{\sqrt{\sqrt{(6 \times .\underline{6})}}}$

vv. $81 = \sqrt{\sqrt{.\underline{1}}}^{(8!+7!)}$ (which is the same as ${}^{-u}\sqrt{\sqrt{\sqrt{.\underline{1}}}}$, where u = 7!/8!)

ww. $56 = (9+.\underline{3}) \times 3!$

xx. $22 = \sqrt{[(6!+6) \times .\underline{6}]}$

110

Brain-Shattering MathDice Puzzles

a. $67 = \sqrt{(8! \div 9+9)}$

b. $21 = \sqrt{(7! \times .7 \div 8)} = 7! \div \sqrt{(8! \div .7)} = 7 \div \sqrt{(.\underline{8}-.\underline{7})}$

c. $11 = 8+6 \div \sqrt{4} = \sqrt{4} \div .\underline{6}+8 = \sqrt{(6 \div \sqrt{.\underline{4}})}+8 = 6+4 \div .8 = (8-.\underline{6}) \div \sqrt{.\underline{4}}$
$= (8-\sqrt{.\underline{4}}) \div .\underline{6}$

d. $27 = \sqrt{\sqrt{.\underline{1}}}^{1-7} = {}^{-.7+.1}\sqrt{.\underline{1}} = {}^{-\sqrt{(.7-\sqrt{.1})}}\sqrt{.\underline{1}}$

e. $33 = \sqrt{4 \div .\underline{06}}$

f. $48 = \sqrt{({}^{.1}\sqrt{2} \div .\underline{2})}$

g. $32 = (7+.\underline{1}) \div .\underline{2} = {}^{-.1}\sqrt{\sqrt{(.7-.2)}}$

h. $96 = \sqrt{({}^{.1}\sqrt{2} \times 9)} = \sqrt{9}!! \times (\sqrt{.\underline{1}}-.2)$

i. $96 = 5!-(\sqrt{16})! = {}^{\sqrt{.1}}\sqrt{6}-5!$

j. $72 = ({}^{-.5}\sqrt{\sqrt{.\underline{1}}})! \div 7! = 5! \times (.7-.1)$

k. $44 = 8 \div .\underline{18}$

l. $39 = (4!+2) \div .\underline{6} = 26 \div \sqrt{.\underline{4}}$

m. $84 = \sqrt{({}^{.2}\sqrt{6}-6!)}$

n. $22 = 33 \times .\underline{6} = \sqrt{[(3!!+3!) \times .\underline{6}]} = (3+.\underline{6}) \times 3! = (3!+.6) \div .3$

o. $55 = (8!-3!!)\div3!!$

p. $58 = \sqrt{[(7!+3!)\times\sqrt{.\underline{4}}]}$

q. $42 = 5!\times.35$

r. $87 = \sqrt{([7!+6)\div\sqrt{.\underline{4}}]}$

s. $36 = {}^{.5}\sqrt{[\sqrt{(5\div.\underline{5})}!]} = \sqrt{[\sqrt{(5/.\underline{5})}!!/.\underline{5}]}$

t. $72 = (5\div.\underline{5})!\div7!$

u. $45 = 7!\div(5!-8) = {}^{-.5}\sqrt{\sqrt{(.8-.\underline{7})}} = 5\div(.\underline{8}-.\underline{7})$

v. $66 = \sqrt{[(6!+6)\times6]}$

w. $21 = \sqrt{(\sqrt{7^6}\div.\underline{7})} = {}^{.6}\sqrt{7}\div\sqrt{.\underline{7}} = .7\div(.7-.\underline{6}) = 7\div\sqrt{(.\underline{7}-.\underline{6})} =$ $(7+7)\div.\underline{6}$

x. $4 = {}^{.7+.8}\sqrt{8} = \sqrt{(8!\div7!+8)} = \sqrt{(7+8\div.\underline{8})} = 7-\sqrt{(8\div.\underline{8})} =$ $\sqrt{[(8!+8!)\div7!]}$

y. $32 = 6!\times.0\underline{4} = \sqrt{4^{6-0!}} = {}^{0!-.6}\sqrt{4}$

z. $18 = {}^{-.5}\sqrt{\sqrt{.0\underline{5}}} = 0!\div(.\underline{5}-.5)$

aa. $56 = ({}^{\sqrt{.1}}\sqrt{2})!\div6! = 6\div.\underline{1}+2 = (6+.\underline{2})\div.\underline{1}$

bb. $45 = 5!\div\sqrt{(7+.\underline{1})} = 7\div.1\underline{5}$

cc. $67 = \sqrt{(8!.\times\underline{1}+9)}$

dd. $48 = \sqrt{(2^9\div.\underline{2})} = 2\times(\sqrt{9!}-2)!$

ee. $84 = \sqrt{[.^2\sqrt{(3!)}-3!!]}$

ff. $45 = \sqrt{[6!\div(.\underline{5}-.2)]} = 5!\div(2+.\underline{6}) = 2\div(.6-.\underline{5})$

gg. $84 = (\sqrt{\sqrt{\sqrt{.2^{-8}}}})!\times.7 = \sqrt{(8!\times.7)}\div2 = \sqrt{[(8!-7!)\times.2]}$

hh. $36 = \sqrt{[7!\div(3+.\underline{8})]} = \sqrt{\sqrt{3!}}\ {}^{8!\div7!}$

ii. $56 = 7\times\sqrt{64} = 7\times\sqrt{\sqrt{4^6}} = 7\times{}^{.6}\sqrt{4} = 7\times(6+\sqrt{4})$

jj. $78 = 5!\times.65$

kk. $84 = 56\div.\underline{6} = \sqrt{(6^5-6!)} = (5!+6)\times.\underline{6} = 5!-6\times6$

ll. $12 = \sqrt{(7!\div35)} = (7-3)!\times.5 = 5!\div(3+7) = \sqrt{[(7-3)!\div5!]} = (7-.\underline{3})\div.\underline{5}$ $= 7!\div3!!+5 = (7-5)\times3! = \sqrt{[(.7-.5)\times3!!]}$

mm. $72 = 8\times3^2 = 8+2^{3!} = .3^{-2}\times8 = 2^{3!}\div.\underline{8} = 8\div(.\underline{3}-.\underline{2}) = 3\times[\sqrt{(2\times8)}]!$ $=\sqrt{(2\times8)}!\div.\underline{3} = 3!!\div(2+8) = (8\div2)!\times3 = (8\div2)!\div.\underline{3} = (\sqrt{\sqrt{2^8}})!\times3 =$ $(\sqrt{\sqrt{2^8}})!\div.\underline{3} = 2\times\sqrt{\sqrt{(3!^8)}}$

111

Two Tiles

These solutions are the best known for each problem. I would be delighted to hear from readers of any possible improvements.

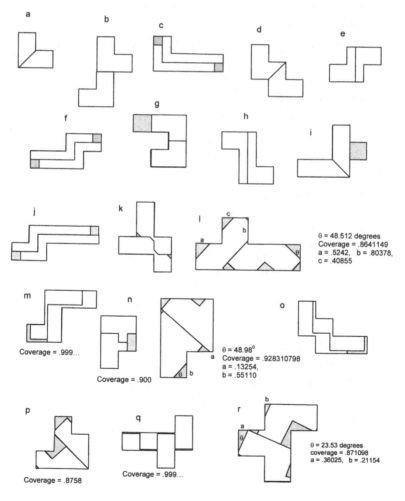

a

b

c

d

e

f

g

h

i

j

k

l

θ = 48.512 degrees
Coverage = .8641149
a = .5242, b = .80378,
c = .40855

m

Coverage = .999...

n

Coverage = .900

θ = 48.98°
Coverage = .928310798
a = .13254,
b = .55110

o

p

Coverage = .8758

q

Coverage = .999...

r

θ = 23.53 degrees
coverage = .871098
a = .36025, b = .21154

112

Three Tiles

These solutions are the best known for each problem. I would be delighted to hear from readers of any possible improvements.

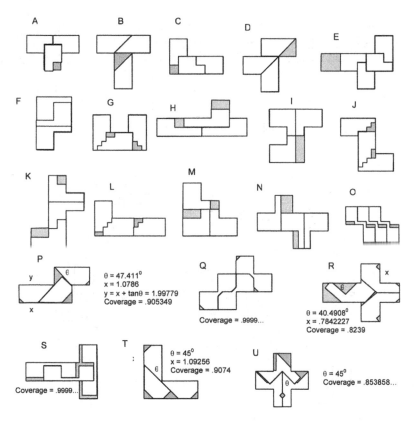

A   B   C   D   E

F   G   H   I   J

K   L   M   N   O

P
y
θ
θ = 47.411°
x = 1.0786
y = x + tanθ = 1.99779
Coverage = .905349

x

Q
Coverage = .9999...

R
x
θ = 40.4908°
x = .7842227
Coverage = .8239

S
Coverage = .9999...

T
θ = 45°
x = 1.09256
Coverage = .9074

U
θ = 45°
Coverage = .853858...

113

Multiple Tiles

These solutions are the best known for each problem. I would be delighted to hear from readers of any possible improvements.

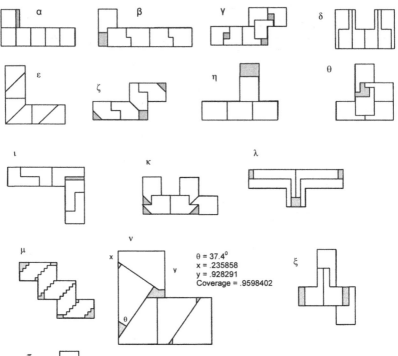

$\theta = 37.4^0$
x = .235858
y = .928291
Coverage = .9598402

114

Three-digit Squares

8		1	6	9		2	2	5		1
4	8	4		6	2	5		7	2	9
1		4	4	1		6	7	6		6

115

Four-digit Squares

2116
1225
1296
6561

116

Number Square

5	4	1
1	4	9
2	1	6

117

Curious License Plate

The license number is 741; the next number is 7425741.

118

Time Equation

(50 min 42 sec) × 9 = 7 hrs 36 min 18 sec.

119

Pi Approximation 1

The best known at the moment are
(a) $.1^{-.5} = 3.1622776...$
(b) $(\sqrt{\sqrt{\sqrt{\sqrt{.9}}}})/(\sqrt{.1}) = 3.14152237...$

120

Pi Approximation 2

The best known at the moment are
(a) Define $a = .8^{.1} = .9779327...$ Define $b = (.3^9/7)^a = 3.7281090(-6)$. Define $c = .5^{-.4}$.
Then $d = 2^c - .6 - b - \pi = 6.598746(-13)$.
(b) The same as the answer in (a) with a 0 added somewhere.

121

Three Consecutive Integers

The following method works to find such examples. Let the numbers be N-1, N, and N+1. Let N+1 = 16k and let N = 27m. Then it's easy to determine that m = 13+16q and k =

22+27q give consecutive integers that are multiples of 27 and 16. Test cases of N-1 for several values of q to find some that are multiples of squares of prime numbers. Examples are 11150 = 446×25, 11151 = 413×27, 11152 = 697×16; 12446 = 254×49, 12247 = 461×27, 12448 = 778×16 or 13310 = 110×121, 13311 = 493×27, 13312 = 832×16. Any cube or fourth powers of primes could be started with other than 27 and 16. The smallest I could find is 1375 = 55×25, 1376 = 172×8, 1377 = 17×81. Another "small" result is 11374 = 94×121, 11375 = 91×125, 11376 = 711×16.

122

Simple Integers

(a) Since 45 is divisible by 9 and 5 the digital sum of any simple integer divisible by 45 must end in 0 and have a digital sum divisible by 9. The smallest is 111111110, the next smallest is 10111111110 and so forth until the 10th smallest is 11111111100. The sum of these ten numbers is 99999999990 so their average plus 1 is 10^{10}.

(b) Since 2439 = 9×271 our simple number must, firstly, have a digital sum divisible by 9. Secondly we note that $10^3 \equiv 187 \bmod(271)$, $10^4 \equiv 244 \bmod(271)$ and $10^5 \equiv 1 \bmod(271)$. This allows us to group digits as follows: A is the sum of digits in places 1, 6, 11,...; B is the sum of digits in places 2, 7, 12,...; C is the sum of digits in places 3, 8, 13,...; D is the sum of digits in places 4, 9, 14,...; and E is the sum of digits in places 5, 10, 15,.... For our simple number to be divisible by both 9 and 271 it must have A+B+C+D+E $\equiv 0 \bmod(9)$ and A+10B+100C+187D+244E $\equiv 0 \bmod(271)$. The smallest solution has ABCDE = 64143 and the smallest simple number divisible by 2439 has 26 digits.

   N = 10000101011110111101111111 =
      2439×4100082415379299344449.

123

Three Interesting Integers

(a) Let $d_N = 100s$ be the digital sum of N_1, and let $d_M = .89d_N$ be the digital sum of $M_1 = N_1 + .1N_1$. If we note that M_1 is computed by adding N_1 to $.1N_1$ (both integers, one shifted by one place relative to the other) we see the digital root of M_1 will be twice d_N less 9 times the number of carries in the addition. Thus $d_M = 89s = 200s - 9c$, which gives $37s = 3c$. The smallest case is $c = 37$ and $s = 3$ giving N_1 with at least 38 digits (the units column won't have a carry) and a digital sum of 300. Thus the minimum possible for N_1 is $N_1 = 909090939999999999999999999999999990 = (90)_3 93(9)_{29} 0$.

(b) Let $d_N = 1000s$ be the digital root of N_2, and let $d_M = .899d_N$ be the digital root of $M_2 = N_2 + .1N_2$. Using the reasoning in part (a) we get $d_M = 899s = 2000s - 9c$, which gives $367s = 3c$. The smallest case is $c = 367$ and $s = 3$ giving the 368-digit number $N_2 = (90)_{33} 93(9)_{299} 0$.

(c) Let $d_N = 10000s$ be the digital root of N_3, and let $d_M = .9001d_N$ be the digital root of $M_3 = N_3 + .1N_3$. Using the reasoning in part (a) we get $d_M = 9001s = 20000s - 9c$, which gives $10999s = 9c$. The smallest case is $c = 10999$ and $s = 9$ giving the 11000-digit number $N_3 = (90)_{999}(9)_{9001} 0$.

ACKNOWLEDGMENTS

I have attempted to identify the source of each puzzle as best I know, and would be happy to hear more on the history of any of the puzzles. So many are passed along by word of mouth and adapted along the way that it's often impossible to determine the true source. Even those published in journals with problem columns often have a history predating their publication.

	Puzzle	Source	Chapter
1	SIX LOGICIANS	Unknown	1
2	FIND THE SECRET MESSAGE	Marvin Miller	1
3	BRIDGE NIGHTMARE	Unknown	1
4	COOPERATIVE BRIDGE	Unknown	1
5	BIRTHDAY GIFT	Unknown	1
6	FOOT RACE	Unknown	1